SCOTCH-IRISH MIGRATION TO SOUTH CAROLINA, 1772

(Rev. William Martin And His Five Shiploads Of Settlers)

By
JEAN STEPHENSON

CLEARFIELD

Originally published
Washington, D.C., 1971

Reprinted for
Clearfield Company, Inc. by
Genealogical Publishing Co., Inc.
Baltimore, Maryland
1999, 2000, 2001, 2002

International Standard Book Number: 0-8063-4832-1

Made in the United States of America

FOREWORD

This book is written primarily for the layman, that is, for the average person interested in history, in knowing something of the background and origin abroad of the men and women who made up the population of this country at the time of the American Revolution. It will also be of value to those of Scotch-Irish origin whose ancestors settled in South Carolina prior to the Revolution, by outlining a procedure whereby in many instances they may be able to identify the general area in Ireland from which their forefathers came.

However, as the story of a nation is but the combined stories of the individuals who make up that nation, it is hoped that the suggestion of a method of identification of those who comprised a significant group of early settlers will prove of interest to historians and stimulate investigation of the origins of similar groups elsewhere, by utilizing comparable records.

The accumulation of data contained herein required many weeks of tedious research and examination of thousands of documents. It would not have been possible without wholehearted cooperation of many persons.

To Mr. Charles E. Lee, Director of the Department of Archives and History of South Carolina, I am indebted for the initial suggestion that the study be made and data compiled, and for constant interest and encouragement thereafter.

Grateful appreciation is also due to Miss Wilma Wates and Mrs. Dolly Law of the staff who with sympathetic attention gave advice on sources of information regarding colonial procedures, customs, and laws, and assisted in tracing obscure references and solving problems of identification of watercourses and place names.

Last, but far from least, my thanks go to all those staff members of the Department of Archives and History of South Carolina who, for weeks at a time, cheerfully brought forth daily truck loads of records for my use.

I also wish to express my appreciation to Mr. Kenneth Darwin, Director of the Ulster Scots Historical Society and Dr. R. J. Dickson for permission to use material from the latter's book, *Ulster Emigration to Colonial America 1718-1775*, and to the former also for a copy of the letter from passengers on the snow *James and Mary* which was published in the *Belfast News Letter*. This furnished corroboration of the conclusion previously reached that the vessel was one of those bringing the Martin party to Charleston.

Jean Stephenson

Washington, D. C.
1970

CONTENTS

CHAPTER 1

SCOTCH-IRISH MIGRATION TO SOUTH CAROLINA

I

A Case Study

This book is the outgrowth of a case study in the identification of the origin of a group of Presbyterian families
who came from the north of Ireland to South Carolina before
the American Revolution.

Because of the great influx of such immigrants between
1740 and the Revolution, the large number of identical first
names and surnames, and the many variations in spelling, it
has been extremely difficult definitely to identify any specific
individual as coming on a specific ship or from a specific area
in Ireland.

Traditions are seldom sufficiently detailed to be of much
help and also, even if specific, usually have not been possible to
document. But a few years ago, in reading, for background
knowledge, the *Council Journals* in the South Carolina Department of Archives and History, full corroboration of a tradition was most unexpectedly found. This led to research on
the group involved, with the results given in this volume.

Similar procedure, carefully followed, as outlined in a
subsequent chapter, will no doubt result in identifying the
general area in Ireland from whence came many other Scotch
Irish families during the late colonial period.

The tradition.- The writer's grandfather, John Calvin
Stephenson, was born in Alabama in 1824 and (as his mother
had died) was reared by his grandparents. They were first
cousins, Hugh M., son of William Stephenson, and Margaret,
daughter of James Stephenson. Both had been born in
Ballymoney, Co. Antrim, Ireland, Hugh on January 25, 1765,

1

and Margaret on November 28, 1770. From them came a detailed account of the family in Scotland and Ireland, as they had heard it from the older generation. Pertinent facts may be summarized as follows:

Robert Stephenson, born in 1723 in Ricalton, Parish of Oxnam, Roxburghshire, Scotland, went to Ireland about 1740-42. There he married and settled at Ballymoney, Co. Antrim. (It should here be mentioned that on the Scottish Border the name, though spelled "Stephenson" since it indicated "son of Stephen", was usually pronounced "Ste'enson" (probably because of the difficulty of giving full value to the "ph" if said rapidly) so is often written as "Steenson" or "Stinson.")

Other members of the Stephenson family were also in the area. About 1768 "Lord Donegail," the absentee landlord, raised the rents to such an extent that even under normal conditions few persons were able to pay without in time exhausting their resources. By 1772 the situation was acute, although those who were employed in the linen industry still had some possessions. These were, however, rapidly being reduced by the necessity of giving aid to their relatives on the farms.

A cousin of Robert Stephenson was married to a man named Beck. Early in 1772 the landlord's agent came to the Beck home, according to tradition, to collect the rent. (It was probably to dispossess them for failure to pay the rent.) It so happened that Mrs. Beck was at a critical stage in having her first child and Mr. Beck (who was a big man, 6 ft. 4 inches and twenty stone, so the story goes) was so concerned about her condition that he could not be bothered and took the bailiff by the neck and threw him out of the house. Unfortunately, the man landed on his head and broke his neck. The wife and baby died; when the authorities came for Mr. Beck he could not be found. He fades out of the picture.

The following Sunday, the minister of the Covenanter Presbyterian Congregation in the area, the Rev. William Martin, preached a sermon on the situation. He stated that every person who knew anything about the country knew the rents were so high that the land would not bring in enough to pay them, that already many were beggared and in time all would be, that human nature being what it was he realized that more and more incidents of the kind that had occurred that week would again occur, but as a minister he could not stand idly by and await the violence and ruin that would come. Steps should be taken "now" to see that such situations did not develop. Therefore he proposed that the congregation pool its resources, that they send to Belfast and charter ships, and the entire congregation, under his leadership, emigrate to South Carolina, where they could get free land and live as free men.

The congregation, having nothing to lose by it, agreed.

The family story goes on to tell how the old man, Robert Stephenson, now a widower, crippled by rheumatism and ill, wanted to go back to see his brothers and sisters, and to die in Scotland, so his young son, Robert, a lad of 15 or 16 years of age, was assigned to take him back to Ricalton. The two older sons, William and James, the eldest daughter Elizabeth and the youngest daughter Nancy (who was engaged to William Anderson and married him before sailing) decided to go to America as proposed by their minister. In addition to his congregation, there were others in the neighborhood who became interested and joined the group. (According to the tradition, after arrival in America this caused some differences of opinion, which led to separation of the Covenanters from the others.)

There were so many to go that all could not be accommodated in one ship (and also some "with means" preferred a ship with more accommodations than those with "no means" could afford). "William Stephenson then had no means, but James Stephenson was still possessed of means," so William's son wrote later.

Four or five ships were needed. They sailed from Belfast, Larne and other ports. All were supposed to sail within a few days of each other but after the ship on which the Stephensons took passage left port the others were delayed and then ran into storms, so when the Stephensons' ship reached Charleston late in October it was first held because of sickness on board and when the passengers finally went ashore they found Rev. William Martin had not arrived and no one knew anything about arrangements for land for them. They had to wait nearly two months until he got there and by that time those who had money had used it up. But soon after he arrived he arranged for their land. However, to their great disappointment, it was not all in one tract, or even adjoining tracts, as they had expected but had to be in individual tracts, scattered all over the colony. Hugh was then seven years old, and Margaret only two, but in their old age they still spoke often of what they had heard from their families and neighbors of incidents during the long voyage and the long wait in Charleston.

So much for the tradition! Now how does it accord with the facts?

In 1939 there was published a list of names of "protestant immigrants to South Carolina" between 1763-1773. [1] However, though the references to the Journals from which taken were given, there was no indication of the connection between those on the various ships or the ports from which they had sailed or any suggestion that the place of settlement in South Carolina could be identified. As there were many persons of the same name definite identification of any one individual has seldom been made.

In recent years, with some of the Draper material on microfilm, and other sources located, there have become available letters and articles written by Daniel Green Stinson (who was born in 1791, son of William Stephenson who had come with the party of Rev. William Martin). Writing to Dr. Lyman Draper, [2] preparing chapters for Mrs. Ellet's use in the third volume of her *Women of the American Revolution*, [3] and her *Domestic History of the American Revolution* [4]

---

[1] Janie Revill, A Compilation of the Original Lists of Protestant Immigrants to South Carolina 1763-1773. (The State Company, Columbia, S. C. 1939).

[2] Draper Papers, VV (microfilm). (Letters dated in the 1870s, quoting from articles printed or written between 1840-1855.)

[3] Elizabeth F. Ellet, The Women of the American Revolution. (New York, 1850.) vol. III (especially p. iv, Preface).

[4] Mrs. Ellet [Elizabeth F.], Domestic History of the American Revolution, (1851), p. 174 et seq.

and in newspaper articles, he gives quite an account of the Rev. William Martin and the migration of his congregation to South Carolina. Numerous articles appearing in various Presbyterian histories and periodicals (hereinafter cited) also refer to it.

As the *Council Journals*, in recording the authorization of surveys for land grants to those who had come with the Rev. William Martin, listed the heads of families under the names of the ships on which they arrived, it became possible (1) to identify the port from which the vessel had sailed, and (2) in many cases the land taken up by each individual—and thus to identify the man for whom the land was surveyed with the port from which that particular man had sailed, and therefore the general area in Ireland from which he came and the time of his leaving, as outlined in Section IV of this chapter.

II

North Ireland on the eve of migration

A recent study of the Scotch-Irish in Ireland and their movement to America, by R. J. Dickson, *Ulster Emigration to Colonial America 1718-1775,*[5] describes in considerable detail the conditions in Ireland between 1740 and 1775. Because of the availability of this volume (to which further reference will be made in Chapter 3), the subject will not be discussed here. Attention is called, however, to the fact that some space is devoted to the expiration in 1770 of the leases of the Earl of Donegall's County Antrim estates and the disturbances and evictions resulting from action taken to raise large sums in connection with the renewal of such leases.[6] This corroborates the tradition of the raise of rents by "Lord Donegail."

The disabilities Presbyterians suffered because of their religion and the depressed condition of the linen trade were burdensome, but they had learned to live under such handi-

---

[5] R. J. Dickson, **Ulster Emigration to Colonial America,** 1718-1775. (Routledge and Kegan Paul, London, 1966; in United States, distributors, Humanities Press, Inc., 303 Park Avenue S., New York, N. Y. 10010.)

[6] Ibid, pp. 74-75.

caps; the excessive rent was the paramount cause for migration at the time Rev. William Martin brought his people to South Carolina. (This theme recurs over and over in the petitions to the Governor for land by those coming from Ireland.)

Thus that portion of the tradition is true—this group, at least, left because they could not afford to remain, and for a place where they could get land virtually "for free," that is, South Carolina.

III

South Carolina: land offered to settlers

The first settlements in South Carolina were along the Coast, and the economy of the first fifty years was to a considerable extent based on rice plantations and slave labor.

Realizing that it would be advantageous for many reasons to have the settlements extend farther inland, where the soil was more suited to other uses and crops, and the increasing population would strengthen the colony, as early as 1731 "poor Protestants" were offered land if they came to the colony to settle. This was on the basis of 100 acres for the head of the family and 50 acres for every other person in the family. Instructions to Governor Lyttelton in 1755 [7] spell out the terms of the grant. The quit rent was to be 4 shillings proclamation money per 100 acres after two years from the date of the grant. When conditions of the grant were fulfilled, the grantee was entitled to another grant on the same basis. The grantee was required to clear and cultivate the land granted at the rate of three acres out of every hundred acres per year.

As an additional encouragement, in 1752 it was provided that there was to be supplied for tools and provisions Five Pounds (£5) proclamation money for each person under 50 and over 12 years of age, and Two Pounds Ten Shillings for each under 12 and over 2 years. [8]

In 1754 a portion of the tax from which was provided the

---

[7] Public Records (South Carolina), vol. XXVI, p. 315 (mss.) in South Carolina Department of Archives and History.
[8] South Carolina Statutes, vol. III, p. 781-782, No. 809, 7 Oct. 1752.

"bounty" mentioned above, was authorized to be used to pay the fees for surveys and grants for such "poor protestants." [9]

There were changes from time to time in these Acts, mostly with respect to the taxes from which they were to be paid but also in the amounts and purposes of payment to the settler.

In July 1761, as the "encouragement heretofore given to poor protestants to become settlers in this province hath not had the desired effect," the bounty was changed. Hereafter, £4 sterling or the value thereof in current money of the Province would be paid to defray the expense of the passage from *Europe* of "every poor free protestant who hath not already received any bounty from this province, and who shall arrive in this province to settle from *Europe* within three years from the passage of this Act above the age of 12 years, and who shall, in case they come from *Great Brittain* or *Ireland,* produce a certificate under the seal of any corporation or a certificate under the hands of the minister and church wardens of any parish, or the ministers and elders of any church, meeting, or congregation, of the good character of such poor protestants above the age of twelve years," and £2 sterling or the equivalent for such poor protestants under twelve and above two years or age brought within the time and for the purpose aforesaid; also twenty shillings sterling or equivalent to such poor protestants above the age of two years, to enable them to purchase tools and provisions. The passage money was to be paid to the owner or master of the vessel unless the emigrant had already paid for his passage, in which case it was paid to him. [10]

This legislation recognized the fact that the cost of transportation was a deterrent to migration and also that not all immigrants had funds with which to procure the type of tools needed to clear land and build a shelter. At the same time, the requirement of references insured settlers of high quality.

The several acts under which these "bounties" were paid

---

[9] South Carolina Statutes, vol. IV, p. 11, No. 826, 11 May 1754.

[10] Acts of the General Assembly of South Carolina passed in the year 1761 (from Microfilm Records of State of South Carolina, Session Laws 1760-1791; taken from Microfilm SC/B.2, Reel 4a, p. 7).

were repealed, amended, or expired from time to time, but were equally often "revived." Ultimately, however, at the close of the term of the General Assembly in 1768 all authority for the payment of bounties finally expired.

News of this spread slowly, however, and for several years thereafter ships continued to bring persons who expected to receive the bounty. (This resulted in a great help to future genealogists, since often their petitions for aid furnish names, both of the petitioners and the ships on which they arrived, and hence their port of embarkation in Ireland can be determined.)

In 1768 the Attorney-General was requested for an opinion on the subject, and his opinion [11] was conclusive that there was no longer authority for the payment of any bounty, but that such "poor protestants" were, however, still entitled to their lands free of charge.

(It should be noted that as late as 1774, emigrants from Ireland arriving to take up lands who did not have funds to go to such lands given them (usually some distance from Charleston) were often given help by the Government and thus, in many cases, there is a record of their names and that of the ships on which they arrived.)

So the group coming with the Rev. William Martin, which arrived late in 1772, were not entitled to a bounty but were possibly entitled to their lands free of charge.

And that brings up the matter of fees.

A person granted land did not get it without any expense, as the fees paid at every step of the procedure could mount up to a considerable sum.

There are numerous references in the statutes and the reports to England as to changes in fees for various transactions but those on the granting of land were remarkably constant. The Commons House of Assembly steadily insisted one of its prerogatives was that of fixing fees. While the fees fixed as early as 1698 were not formally approved by the

King, Governor Bull stated in 1764 [12] that most officers "conformed thereto."

These were as follows——

Fees: [13]

	Pounds	shillings	pence
To the Surveyor General—			
For running a line, per acre			4
For a plat, certificate and copy	2.	10.	—
For an attested copy of a plat		30.	—
For a warrant		2.	6
For a copy of a warrant and precept endorsed thereon		10.	—
To the Deputy Surveyor—			
For each day he has to ride to place to be surveyed and back, if over 20 miles		50.	—
To the Governor—			
For a warrant		2.	6
For a grant of 500 acres or under		10.	—
if over 500 acres	1.	—	—
To the Secretary—			
For a warrant		2.	6
For filing the surveyor's certificate		1.	—
For a grant of 500 acres or under		10.	—
For a grant of over 500 acres		15.	—

Of course, the amount paid depended on the requirements in each case, but even if the Deputy Surveyor did not have to travel far or often, the total sum might well be as much as Five Pounds, a considerable sum in those days.

The procedure followed in acquiring land may be of interest.

Persons who applied for land had to appear in person before the Governor in Council, and make their request, show they were of good character and in condition to improve the land by settling on it, etc. If the Governor was satisfied on these points and therefore decided the person was entitled to land, such fact was recorded in the *Council Journal* and the preparation of a warrant for survey was directed.

The person receiving the warrant took it to the Surveyor General, who prepared an attested copy with a general precept

[12] Bull to Board of Trade, 21 December 1764; British Record Office, XXX 234.

[13] Thomas Cooper, ed., **The Statutes at Large of South Carolina** (Columbia, S. C., 1838) vol. III, p. 346.

endorsed thereon, and gave it to the person presenting the warrant—after the fee was paid to him, of course.

That person then took the attested copy and precept to the appropriate deputy surveyor, who made the survey, prepared a plat, endorsed the warrant and gave the survey and plat to the person taking up land, again after payment of the fees.

That person, within 30 days, returned the survey and plat to the Surveyor General's office (on penalty of land being declared vacant).

The Surveyor General within 20 days would certify and deliver the plats. The person for whom the survey had been made could then apply to the Secretary of the Province for a grant.

* * * * *

North of Ireland families, and some from elsewhere in Ireland, flocked to a colony that advertised for and wanted settlers who were willing to work hard if they were allowed to have security in their lands and to be free to have their own churches. The migration began with a trickle in 1750, became a flood in the 1760s, and while it slackened somewhat after the bounties were terminated, still continued up to the beginning of the Revolution. Even after the Revolution, during the latter part of the century, individuals and small parties continued to come from Ireland into South Carolina.

IV

Identification Procedure

The problem has always been to distinguish between persons of the same name, some of whom may have come directly from Ireland and some by way of Pennsylvania or Virginia. But as most of those coming from Ireland applied at once and in groups they can usually, by sufficient study, be identified.

The steps taken to determine the general location in Ireland from whence came the settlers on the five ships carrying the Rev. William Martin's party will be outlined in detail herein.

In this case, the known facts as to a large number of the

emigrants on these ships being his congregation and their friends made it possible to work in both directions — back toward origin in Ireland, forward toward place of settlement in South Carolina. (For suggestions as to procedure for tracing others *back* from the residence in South Carolina of the ancestor, see Chapter 5.)

In compiling this identification of the settlers in Rev. William Martin's group the purpose has NOT been to trace descendants or even definitely to identify these immigrants after their arrival in South Carolina, but instead to demonstrate the use of various types of records (newspapers, surveys, grants, ship arrivals, ports of sailing, diaries, ecclesiastical records and histories, histories of specific areas here and abroad, etc.) to determine the origin abroad of settlers here during the colonial period.

The key factor in this case was Rev. William Martin, as leader of the group. As shown in Chapter 3, he is so referred to in the *Council Journal*.

This is further documented by numerous references to Rev. William Martin in Presbyterian periodicals, [14] as well as in the letters and articles of Daniel Green Stinson, and statements of those who, as children, came with the party.

In the *Council Journal*, names are given of the following ships: the *Lord Dunluce, Hopewell, Pennsylvania Farmer*, and *Free Mason*, and another group of persons listed (prior to the *Free Mason* group) without giving the name of the ship on which they came.

A search of the Charleston, South Carolina, newspapers from midsummer 1772 to mid-January 1773 showed arrival of five ships from north Ireland ports at the right time, furnished names of the captains and port from which they sailed, and these ports were all those from which passengers from the Ballymoney area might logically have embarked. Four of these ships were the *Lord Dunluce, Hopewell, Penn-*

---

[14] Among them: William Glasgow, "Sketches of the Ministry of the Reformed Church in America, No. 3, William Martin," Reformed Presbyterian Church and Covenanter, vol. XXIV (1886), p. 400. Rev. James McConnell, Fasti of the Irish Presbyterian Church, 1613-1840. Revised by Rev. S. G. McConnell; Appendix, American Section; Ministers of Irish Origin who Laboured in America During the Eighteenth Century, compiled by Rev. David Stewart. Belfast, 1943.

sylvania Farmer, and *Free Mason*. The fifth was the snow, *James and Mary*, which sailed from the same port as the *Lord Dunlunce*, and, as will be seen later, passengers on it are known from several other sources to have been part of Rev. William Martin's party.

The authorization for surveys of land were issued to persons grouped by the ship in which they came, except in one case where the name of the ship is not given. Further investigation showed the authorizations for persons on the unnamed ship were all dated December 11 and included persons known from other sources to be in the Rev. William Martin's party, and while dated December 11, the names of the individuals to whom they were to be issued were not entered in the *Council Journal* until January 6, when they were entered with the others of the Rev. William Martin's party. Apparently, the sequence of events was as follows: The *James and Mary* arrived long before the rest of the ships (stating others would follow), was detained for some time in quarantine because of smallpox having been on board; then persons on it applied for the bounty and land, were refused bounty but after some delay surveys were authorized and apparently warrants and precepts prepared December 11 but not issued, nor were the names of the individuals entered in the *Council Journal* until after the arrival of the Rev. William Martin.

This sequence of events, compiled from contemporary accounts, is identical with the tradition with respect to early arrival, illness on board, delay in getting land until arrival of Rev. William Martin, etc.

The names of all individuals on the five ships *for whom surveys were authorized have been checked* against surviving surveys and some 80% identified. Doubtless more could be found by checking all variations in spelling (i.e., Ervine, Irvine, Irving, Erwin; Rork, O'Rourke, McRook; Galispy, Gillespie, etc., see Chapter 6).

At the time the surveys were made and until 1785, the county unit as now known did not exist in South Carolina. True, in 1682, three "counties" were laid out. Roughly, the locations were from points along the coast as follows, the line extending up fairly straight, though probably following the rivers to some extent—

Craven County: From the North Carolina line to Seewee Creek (present Awendaw Creek) emptying into Bull's Bay.

Berkeley County: From Seewee Creek to the Stono River.

Colleton County: From the Stono River to the Combahee River.

Later another was added: Granville County, from the Combahee to the Savannah.

These names were continued in use until after the Revolution, but largely merely as a means of locating lands granted or sold and as the jurisdiction of militia units.

In 1769, Judicial Districts were created. Along the coast and extending about fifty miles inward were three —

Georgetown, from the North Carolina line to the Santee River.

Charleston, between the Santee and the Combahee River.

Beaufort, between the Combahee and the Savannah Rivers.

Above these were the remaining districts—

Cheraws, above Georgetown, bounded on the west by Lynches River.

Camden, west of Cheraws, bounded on the west by the Santee-Congaree-Broad River system.

Between Camden District and the Savannah River was divided into two districts.

Orangeburg was the southern one.

Ninety-six was the northern one.

For a good description of the changing names of counties, districts, etc., see *South Carolina Historical Magazine*, vol. 69, page 155.

It was not until 1785 that the county system as we know it now was set up, and records kept in the counties.

The statement in the survey that the land was in a certain county therefore does not indicate it was in the county of the same name at present. However, by means of identifying the watercourses mentioned in a survey and by checking the location of abuting owners, in many cases it has been possible to determine the county in which the land fell in 1785, and so the courthouse in which records thereafter made affecting such land may be located. It could be determined for most of the other cases by completing such research.

The land grants made as a result of the surveys have not been examined. Such examination may aid in further identification of the subsequent county in which the land was located.

By examination of the *General Index of Wills of Counties of South Carolina* (typescript in South Carolina Department of Archives and History), names identical with those of some of the persons taking up land under these surveys were found in the counties in which their surveys had been located. Such wills were examined and when there was reasonable identification of the maker of the will with the person taking up the survey a brief abstract of the will was made. Enough of these were so located to indicate it would be worthwhile for one descended from or interested in a person of the name of one taking up a listed survey to have a thorough search made in the records of the county in which the land covered by the survey was located for a deed (to see if the identical land was sold by such person or by his children) and if none, for the will, administration or settlement of estate of such person, etc., and thus determine whether the person concerned is actually the person for which the search is being made.

The index of deeds for a few of the counties in which surveys were located was examined for deeds by a *grantor* bearing names of "Martin party immigrants" who had surveys in such counties, as some of them no doubt sold the land sooner or later. Such deeds were examined and when the land sold appeared from the description to cover the land that had been surveyed for such person, abstract of the deed was made.

A few "spot checks" were made of other records and when such record appeared to refer to a "Martin party immigrant" a note was made of such record.

The results of this research appear in Chapter 3, Section

II, following the abstract of the survey and note of the county.

It should be borne in mind that no attempt was made to do any research on most of the names of persons listed as coming on these five ships, nor exhaustive research on *any* of the names listed.

It should also be remembered that these are NOT passenger lists but lists of those who *applied* for land grants. It is known that some persons who came on these ships bought their land and did not apply for grants; also some who applied for grants never went any further, and did not have a survey made.

In some cases no doubt a survey plat was prepared but cannot now be found. However, in such cases, there still may be available the subsequent grant. Rev. William Martin took up a grant, but also bought much additional land. Others may have done the same.

What has been done demonstrates that it will not be difficult to establish the identity of the first and probably the second generation in this country of a large percentage of this group of immigrants. The majority of them were probably from the vicinity of Ballymoney, Ballymena, Kellswater, and Vow, County Antrim. Those who can *prove* descent from such a person will know the general area in Ireland in which to begin the search for the immigrant ancestor abroad and his antecedents.

For this purpose the maps and general information in *Ulster Emigration to Colonial America, 1718-1775* will be most helpful. It is recommended that it be read carefully before work in Ireland is initiated. (See Footnote 5.)

CHAPTER 2

REV. WILLIAM MARTIN: HIS CHURCH

AND HIS CAREER

No one has made a careful study of the career of William Martin, the first Covenanting minister in South Carolina; nevertheless considerable information is available. As his name is mentioned in nearly all accounts of Scotch-Irish settlers in South Carolina in the last quarter of the 18th century, a brief sketch of his career will be of interest.

The only positive statement of his parentage at present available is from the University of Glasgow, where the record reads—

"No. 1612. *Gulielmus Martin, filus natu maximus Davidus Martin in Com. de Londonderry,* Minister of the Irish Reformed Presbyterian Church; ordained at Vow, near Rasharkin 1757." [1]

Thus it can be accepted that he was the eldest son of David Martin of Londonderry.

He was born at Ballyspollum, near Ballykelly, Co. Londonderry, Ireland, 16 May 1729. [2]

It is sometimes stated that he was born in the Parish of Loughgilly [Loughguile], Co. Antrim, Ireland, 16 May 1731, and "was reared in the strictest manner by Covenanter parents." [3] The last part of this statement is no doubt correct; the first was found to be an error and corrected later but, as is well known, an error once in print is copied and recopied. The articles giving the differing dates were writ-

---

[1] W. Innes Addison, **Matriculation Album of the University of Glasgow, 1728-1850,** p. 50.

[2] W. Melancthon Glasgow, **History of the Reformed Presbyterian Church in America** (Baltimore 1888), p. 572.

[3] W. M. Glasgow, "Sketch of the Ministry of the Reformed Presbyterian Church in America, No. 3—William Martin," **Reformed Presbyterian and Covenanter,** vol. XXIV (1886).

17

ten by the same man, the first quoted above (Londonderry) published two years *after* the second one (Antrim), with the statement "Information received from Ireland."

There was a David Martin of Mois (Mays), Co. Londonderry, whose family was settled in the Parish of Templemore, that county, as early as the 1650s, and it should be noted that in the matriculation record at Glasgow, William was stated to be the son of a David of Londonderry. The printed records of the Parish of Templemore (1634-1703) contain many references to this family. The unprinted records from 1704 are complete and are in the vaults of the Cathedral at Londonderry. [4]

Presbyterians in Ireland were first slowly organized into "societies," which then associated themselves into corresponding meetings and these into a General Meeting.

When, in 1743, the Reformed Presbytery (Covenanter) was constituted many of the North Ireland people submitted to it. Several "missionary" ministers preached at various places. But this ceased when the Presbytery was disrupted in 1753, and for a few years there was no Covenanter minister there. About this time William Martin, who was educated at the University of Glasgow, began the study of theology under Rev. John McMillan and was licensed by the Reformed Presbytery of Scotland 10 October 1756. He soon returned to Ireland and was ordained at Vow, near Rasharkin, Co. Antrim, 2 July 1757, and placed in charge of the societies centering in Ballymoney 13 July 1757. [2]

He became active in establishing the "Covenanter" Presbyterian Church in Ireland. In time several other ministers were ordained, at which ceremony he usually officiated. [5] At first the members were scattered and formed into small societies and each minister had several under his care. In 1760, the societies in the southeastern part of Ulster were divided into two congregations, separated by the River Bann.

---

[4] I am indebted for this information to Mrs. Margaret Dickson Falley, who examined such records during research in Ireland for her book, Irish and Scotch-Irish Ancestral Research (privately printed, 1962), p. 178.
[5] Rev. Samuel Ferguson, Biographical Sketches of Some Irish Covenanting Ministers (1897) pp. 13, 19, 29, 93.

Martin chose the Kellswater congregation and lived at Bangor for many years. [2]

By 1763 there was sufficient Covenanting ministers to form the Presbytery of Ireland; William Martin was, of course, a member. [6]

Conditions became steadily worse for the Presbyterians in Northern Ireland. Not only were they taxed to support a church not their own but most of them were either employed in some branch of the textile industry or were farmers. Business was bad in one and rents too high in the other. Activities of agents during the period that South Carolina offered a bounty to settlers had resulted. in considerable migration, so it was not an unfamiliar undertaking by 1772.

About this time Rev. William Martin received a "call" to come to South Carolina. [7] Presbyterian tradition is that he decided to go and, following an incident of violence resulting from high rents, he preached a sermon calling on all his congregation to accompany him. Whether this is true or not is immaterial, since the facts are clear that he did go and took with him a party of some 467 families on five ships. In fact, "Rev. William Martin (Kellswater)" is shown as one of the agents in signing up the passengers for the *Lord Dunluce*, on which he sailed. [8]

About 1750 some Presbyterians from Octoraro in eastern Pennsylvania, Virginia and North Carolina had come to South Carolina and settled on Rocky Creek. By 1755 emigrants from Ireland were coming in—many being Covenanters.

After some years the five or six Presbyterian groups (Associate, Covenanter, Burgher, Anti-Burgher, Seceders, etc.) combined to build a union Church, which they called "Catholic" as all groups were to worship there. It was located "on the Rocky Mount Road, 15 miles southeast of Chester." Rev. William Richardson, of Waxhaws, was for a time the

[6] "Historical Sketch of the Reformed Church in Ireland (from the Reformed Presbyterian Magazine, Edinburgh)," The Covenanter, vol. XII (1856), p. 262.
[7] W. Melancthon Glasgow, History of the Reformed Presbyterian Church in America. (Baltimore, Md. 1888.) p. 380.
[8] R. J. Dickson, Ulster Emigration to Colonial America 1718-1775 (London, 1966), p. 254.

preacher.   In 1770, the Covenanters began to hold society meetings, and soon wrote to Ireland for a minister. [7]

It was partly in response to this call that Rev. William Martin came to South Carolina, the first Covenanter minister settled in the south.   While, as will be seen, the party he brought could not get their lands together, many were able to settle in the Rocky Creek area, where their leader located. He not only took up land by grant in 1773 (see Chapter 4) but bought a square mile (640 acres) and built a stone house on it. [9]

At first he preached at Catholic regularly.   In 1774 the Covenanter congregation withdrew from Catholic and built a log church on the same road as the Catholic church and two miles east of it, "on the dividing ridge between Great and Little Rocky Creeks." [9]   (This was described in 1876 as being near the house of Mrs. James Barbour Ferguson. [10]) There he preached to his own congregation.

In early years the Revolutionary War did not particularly affect the settlers in the area, but by 1780 the situation changed.   In that year the British and the Tories were ranging the country.   Mr. Martin then preached a sermon described vividly by Dr. Latham and (probably with some added "romantic touches") in Mrs. Ellet's *Domestic History of the American Revolution*. [11]   There are several accounts of this sermon, written some 30 to 60 years later, but all purporting to be based on conversations with those present.   While differing in the phraseology used, all have the same theme and agree on the sense of what he said.   They may be summed up by saying that he reminded the congregation of the hardships their fathers had suffered, in religion and in their possessions, that they had been forced out of Scotland, had been forced out of Ireland, had come over to America and

[9] W. Melancthon Glasgow, History of the Reformed Presbyterian Church in America (Baltimore, Md. 1888) p. 388; Mrs. E. F. Ellet, Domestic History of the American Revolution (1851) ; Rev. R. Latham, A Historical Sketch of Union A. R. Church, Chester Co., S. C. (Chester, S. C., 1888).

[10] "Sketch of Covenanters on Rocky Creek, S. C., from Chester (S.C.) Reporter," in The Reformed Presbyterian Church and Covenanter, combined series, vol. XIV (1876), pp. 171-177.

[11] Rev. R. Latham, D.D., A Historical Sketch of Union A. R. Church, Chester Co., S. C. (Chester, S. C. 1888) pp. 33-34; Mrs. Ellet, Domestic History of the American Revolution (1851).

cleared their lands and built their homes and their church and were free men; that now the British were coming in, and soldiers would again be depriving them of the fruits of their labors and be driving them out. They should not stand meekly and idly by while all they had wrought was taken from them; there was a time to pray and a time to fight, and the time to fight had come!

On the conclusion of the sermon, he ended the meeting. Two companies were immediately formed under Ben Land and under Captain Barbour, [12] and agreed to rendezvous with arms and horses the following day. They did so, and promptly joined the American forces attempting to repulse the British.

As a result of the sermon, the British soon after burned the church. They also took Martin prisoner. [13] He was confined for six months in Rocky Mount and Camden. Then he was taken before Lord Cornwallis, together with Col. Winn who had been recently captured. Some months earlier Col. Winn's men had captured several Loyalist officers, among them Col. John Phillips, who had come from Ireland in 1770 and settled on Jackson Creek. The men had wanted to kill Col. Phillips and the others captured but Col. Winn would not permit them to do so. Later Col. Phillips had been exchanged for Col. David Hopkins. [14]

Fortunately for Martin and Winn, Col. Phillips was now on Lord Cornwallis' staff and was present when they were brought in. Of course, he felt under some obligation to Col. Winn, and it developed that he had kept the race horses of Lord Cornwallis' father in Ireland and there had known Rev. William Martin "and respected him." There are several accounts of the interview with Lord Cornwallis, one of which quotes Martin as saying, "I was raised in Scotland; educated

---

[12] Captain Barbour has not been definitely identified. One of that name appears to have been captain of a North Carolina company. As Martin was a favorite minister of the Presbyterians and preached in the Waxhaw settlement from time to time, and some of his Congregation in Chester are known to have served in North Carolina companies, it is possible that this particular Captain Barbour had come down to hear him, and do a little recruiting on the side. No attempt has been made to identify these companies. From statements made in subsequent applications for pensions, it is quite probable that no formal company records were kept.

[13] W. M. Glasgow, "Sketch of the ministry of the Reformed Presbyterian Church in America," Reformed Presbyterian and Covenanter (1886) XXIV, p. 400.

[14] E. A. Jones, ed., Journal of Alexander Chesney, a South Carolina Loyalist in the Revolution and after, (Columbus (Ohio) 1921) p. 61.

in its library and theological schools, was settled in Ireland where I spent the prime of my days and emigrated to this country seven years ago." [15]

We have no further details. However, the result was that they were released. It would appear that either a condition of his release was that Rev. William Martin would not return to Chester Co., or else because of extreme Tory activity in Chester Co. it was felt that it was unwise for him to return there, for he went to Mecklenburg Co., North Carolina.

Rev. William Martin remained in Mecklenburg Co., definitely a Presbyterian stronghold, until after the surrender at Yorktown. Then he returned to Chester Co. His "log church" had been burned down, so he took charge of the congregation at Catholic.

When, in 1782, the Covenanter ministers Cuthbertson, Dobbin and Linn in Pennsylvania joined with other groups of Presbyterians to form the Associate Reformed Presbyterian Church he refused to go into it with them. That left him the only Covenanter minister in America "who professed to teach the whole doctrine of the Reformation, and who kept alive the Covenanter Church in America." [16]

Whether this difference of opinion on doctrine had anything to do with it is not known, but in 1785 he was dismissed by the Catholic congregation for intemperance. As one writer phrased it, "He was somewhat less temperate than became him in the use of strong drink." [17] Others insisted that during cold weather everyone was offered whiskey on arrival at a house, and he took no more than anyone else. Even though he knew it was being stated he overindulged, he refused to permit others to dictate what he should do, so continued to accept liquor when offered. There are several statements by men who knew him that they never had seen him when he had too much. The argument raged for many years after his death.

Though dismissed from that congregation he did not cease preaching and apparently his services were in great demand.

[15] George Howe "History of the Presbyterian Church in South Carolina," Reformed Presbyterian and Covenanter, IV (1877) p. 58.
[16] Sketch of Ecclesiastical History, printed by J. Smythe (Belfast 1818) p. 109.
[17] Mrs. E. F. Ellet, Domestic History of the American Revolution (1851) p. 124.

During the next few years he preached at school houses, at Edward McDaniel's, down to Jackson Creek, at Richard Gladney's in Fairfield, across the Catawba at William Hicklen's "who had moved from Rocky Creek to Lancaster Co." [18] He also supplied the Society at Long Cane in Abbeville Co. [19] "His preaching during that dreary period did much to keep alive the Covenanting cause." [20]

One account of him stated that his congregation in the Rocky Creek area then built him another church, east of the one burnt down, on the Rocky Mount Road, on a beautiful hill in a grove of trees. There he preached until his death. [18]

In 1791 Rev. James McGarragh was sent as a missionary by the Reformed Presbytery of Ireland, and settled in the Beaver Dam Society. In 1792 Rev. William King was sent out by the Scottish Presbytery. Mr. Martin was then preaching at Jackson Creek, Wolf Pit Meeting House, Winnsboro, and in private homes at many settlements between Statesville, N. C. and Louisville, Georgia. Messrs. Martin, McGarragh, and King were formed in 1793 into a committee of the Reformed Presbyterian Church of Scotland to manage the affairs of the church in America, thus perpetuating the Reformed Presbytery.

As might have been expected, things were not harmonious in the committee. All were strong, positive men, with differing backgrounds. Martin, of the "gentry" class, had all his life been the leader in his area and in his church; he probably did not accept advice from younger men. Within a few years the committee was dissolved by Mr. Martin withdrawing at a time when the remaining two members of the Presbytery were preparing charges against him, on the grounds that he had been intoxicated three times, had sold a negro and so would not be in a position to free him if the church decided such should be done, and had not properly administered a matter of church discipline. [21] He and his

---

[18] "Covenanters on Rocky Creek, S. C.," The Reformed Presbyterian and Covenanter, combined series, XIV (1876), pp. 171-177.
[19] The Covenanter, IV, p. 217.
[20] Rev. D. D. Faris, "Reminiscences of the Reformed Presbyterian Church in South Carolina," The Reformed Presbyterian and Covenanter, XIV (1876), pp. 52 et seq.
[21] W. Melancthon Glasgow, History of the Reformed Church in America (Baltimore, Md. 1888), pp. 572 et seq.

congregation ignored the charges and all attacks on him, and he continued to preach to his own congregation and to administer baptism until his death.

Writing in 1888, Dr. Latham said, with reference to these charges, "It would have been regarded, three-quarters of a century ago, as breach of the laws of civilized society for a parishioner not to have furnished his preacher with some kind of spirits when he came to visit him, either socially or ministerially. It was, no doubt, when out visiting his Scotch-Irish neighbors, and enjoying their unbounded hospitality, that Mr. Martin became intoxicated. With all his faults or rather with this one fault, William Martin was a Christian gentleman and a patriot of the purest type. He made an impress for good on Rocky Creek which is felt to this day. His influence over the Covenanters was unbounded, and at his bidding they rose in their solid might to redeem what appeared to many, a lost cause." [22]

About 1804 the stone house he had built in 1774 burned down. He then built a log cabin nearby, in which he lived the rest of his life.

In 1806 he was injured by a fall from his horse, resulting in a fever, from which he died 25 October 1806. He was buried in a small graveyard near his cabin. "He was a large, fine looking man, a proficient scholar, and eloquent preacher, and an able divine." [21]

Prior to his death he had given much of his land to his nephews, William and David Martin and Hugh Wilson. [23]

William Martin married first Mary ———, who died in Ireland; [24] second, Jenny Cherry, in Ireland, about 1771, [22] and third, Susanna ———, who survived him. [25]

His only daughter, who married John McCaw of York Co., predeceased him, [26] leaving issue. McCaw later moved with his family to Randolph Co., Illinois. [27]

[22] Rev. R. Latham D.D., A Historical Sketch of Union A. R. Church, Chester County, South Carolina (1888), p. 40.
[23] Chester Co., S. C., Deed Boook G, pp. 213, 256 257.
[24] Mrs. E. F. Ellet, Domestic History of the American Revolution (1851) p. 181.
[25] Chester Co., S. C., Deed Book G, p. 257.
[26] "Sketch of Covenanters on Rocky Creek," from Chester (S. C.) Reporter, in The Reformed Presbyterian and Covenanter, vol. XIV (1876), pp. 171-177.
[27] Rev. D. S. Faris, "Reminiscences of the Reformed Presbyterian Church in South Carolina," The Reformed Presbyterian and Covenanter, vol. XIV (1876) p. 52.

CHAPTER 3

CONGREGATION OF REV. WILLIAM MARTIN IN
IRELAND AND MIGRATION TO
SOUTH CAROLINA

I

In Ireland

The Stephenson tradition, supported by letters and memoirs of a son of one of the immigrants, and early statements on Presbyterianism in South Carolina, is that the congregation of the Rev. William Martin came with him from Ballymoney, which is a town in Co. Antrim, Ireland. This seems to be true, but it is also true that there were in Ballymoney other congregations of Presbyterians, and members of these groups were in the party coming with him.

The Presbyterians in Ireland were divided into several "sects," which differed from each other in matters of doctrine as well as in their attitude toward cooperation (or lack of it) with the civil government.

At Ballymoney the Presbyterian Church of Ireland established a congregation as early as 1646, but the charge was vacant (i.e., there was no minister there) from August 1768 until after August 1772. [1]

As early as 1748 the Seceders (a "splinter" Presbyterian group) recognized their members in "Ballyreshane, Derrykeghen, Ballymoney, and Kilroughts" as forming a "collegiate," that is each was not sufficiently organized to maintain a settled minister but, as grouped, constituting a charge. [2]

---

[1] James Seaton Reid, History of the Presbyterian Church in Ireland, with biographical notices of eminent Presbyterian ministers and laymen, with Introduction and notes by Rev. W. D. Killen (Edinburgh, 1886), p. 43.

[2] Rev. David Stewart, The Seceders in Ireland, p. 75.

Yet members of the Reformed Presbyterian Church (Covenanter) were there prior to 1757; it was this group of which Rev. William Martin was minister.

Thus when Rev. William Martin suggested the migration to South Carolina it seems probable (from later differences) that members of all three groups came in his party. It may be significant that after 1772 the Seceders and Reformed groups remaining in the Ballymoney area were too small to support a minister and after the death in 1799 of the minister of the Presbyterian Church of Ireland who was installed in 1772, the remaining members of that congregation were taken into the congregation of Ballymena.

Although it is quite likely that the majority of his party were from Ballymoney or vicinity, it seems probable that persons from other areas may have joined the group. Suggestions as to such areas may be obtained from a study of the chapter on "Ports and Agents" and the names and locations of owners and agents listed in Advertisements of Sailings in *Ulster Emigration to Colonial America, 1718-1775.* [3]

No mention has thus far been found in Irish sources available in the United States of the Beck incident or of the resulting sermon of Rev. William Martin, but there is mention that he had a "call" to South Carolina. [4] Many references are made in works on early Presbyterianism in the colonies to the fact that he "came with his own people" to South Carolina in 1772. [5] There seems to be little reason to doubt that he was the instigator of the movement. At all events, it was decided they should go.

In the congregation was Robert Stephenson (Ste'enson, Stinson), a widower with three sons, James, William and Robert and two daughters, Elizabeth (married to Alexander Brady) and Nancy. According to statements of his grandson, the father, Robert, was in poor health and wanted to return to Scotland, and the teen-aged son Robert took him back to his old home in Scotland. The family tradition states

[3] R. J. Dickson, Ulster Emigration to Colonial America, 1718-1775 (London, 1966).
[4] R. J. Dickson, Ulster Emigration to Colonial America, 1718-1755 (London, 1966) p. 248. (Advertisement in Belfast News Letter, 16 June 1772.)
[5] W. M. Glasgow, "Sketches of the ministry of the Reformed Presbyterian Church in America, No. 3, William Martin," Reformed Presbyterian and Covenanter, vol. XXIV (1886), p. 400.

that *the other four came with Rev. William Martin's party.* However, the records show that Alex. Brady was already in South Carolina, and in the area where the Stephensons settled. [6] His wife, Elizabeth, does not appear in the list of those of the Martin party applying for land, so she may have accompanied her husband earlier, or, as she was merely coming to rejoin her husband and he had already taken up the land to which he was entitled and did not need more, she was a passenger but does not appear on the list of applicants for land.

The old man, Robert, and his young son, Robert, returned to Scotland. [7] The two married sons, James and William, with their families, and the daughter, Nancy, who married William Anderson before sailing, and probably the daughter Elizabeth, were part of the Martin party.

There were, of course, many problems as to ships, etc. The ships on which they sailed were identified from the *Council Journals* and the Charleston newspapers. Subseqently, with the publication in 1966 of Dr. Dickson's volume on Ulster Emigration [8] some interesting information taken from the advertisements in the Belfast newspaper is available, as follows:

James and Mary: 200 tons; master, J. Workman; agents, Jas. McVicker, John Moore, merchant. On July 29, hoped that passengers would be punctual and allow vessel to sail Aug. 8. Finally sailed from Larne Aug. 25, 1772.

———————

[6] The South Carolina Council Journal (No. 36 part 2, p. 141), 20 July 1772, under "Petitions for land admitted to be read," lists over 100 names, including, on p. 144, "Alex'r Brady ———— 100 acres." This land was surveyed for him 7 Sept. 1772, 299 acres on small branch of Rocky Creek in Craven Co., bd'd by Alexander McKane, Sarah McKane, Jane Miller, Mary Wade, Robert Wilson, and vacant land. (Pre-Revolutionary Plat Book, vol. 12, p. 193.)

[7] It was the intention that after the death of Robert, Sr., the young son, Robert, would come to South Carolina to join his brothers, but the father survived several years and then the outbreak of the American Revolution prevented the journey. By the time it was over he was married and working to support a family, so the brothers were never united. However, as the last surviving member of each generation, on each side of the ocean, died, the word of such death was written to the relatives on the other side until 1936 when the writer of this book received word of the death of Thomas St. Lawrence Stephenson from the latter's stepson. He was the last survivor of the Scottish-English branch of the family. (The son Robert had crossed into England and settled there. He was the father of George Stephenson, inventor of the locomotive, and several others including Ann (b. 1781, died 1840) who married John Nixon, and came with him to the United States in the early 1800s, settling in Pittsburgh, Penna. Nixon was later captain on Ohio River steamboats.)

[8] R. J. Dickson, Ulster Emigration to Colonial America, 1718-1755, p. 253, James and Mary; p. 254, Lord Dunluce; p. 248, Hopewell, Pennsylvania Farmer; p. 252, Freemason.

Lord Dunluce: 400 tons; Master, Jas. Gillis; agent, John Montgomery, merchant, Rev. Wm. Martin (Kellswater), Wm. Barklie (Ballymena on Saturdays). On Aug. 28 advertised that passengers should give earnest before Sept. 5 as more offered to go than can be taken; but on Sept. 15 announced some families drawn back so can accommodate 200 passengers more. The ship finally sailed from Larne Oct. 4, 1772.

Pennsylvania Farmer: 350 tons; Master, C. Robinson; agent, John Ewing, S. Brown, merchants; later added Rev. John Logue (Broughshane). Sailing postponed to allow farmers to dispose of their crops; sailed from Belfast Oct. 16, 1772.

Hopewell: 250 tons. June 16 advertised arrival in England from South Carolina; a minister urgently needed. [9] Advertised Master, J. Ash; agent, Wm. Beatty, merchant; sailed from Belfast, with Capt. Martin, Master, Oct. 19, 1772.

Free Mason: 250 tons. Master, John Semple; agent, J. W. & G. Glenry, Hill Wilson, Geo. Anderson, Wm. Booth, merchants, owners. Sailed from Newry 27 Oct. 1772.

In the chapter entitled "The Voyage to America," in *Ulster Emigration to Colonial America*[3] Dr. Dickson gives a vivid description of the conditions on vessels plying between north Ireland ports and America, so it will not be discussed here, except to say that it was a voyage of some seven to nine weeks to Charleston. Of course, if infectious fever or smallpox broke out on board there would also be a quarantine period.

For conditions in Ireland leading to the migration and for further information on localities in Ireland from which vessels sailing from the ports named drew their passengers, see *Ulster Emigration to Colonial America, 1718-1775.*[3]

II

Arrival in South Carolina

The arrival of the vessels in South Carolina is shown in the newspapers. *The South Carolina Gazette,* issue of 22

---

[9] As the advertisement on June 16 states a minister is urgently needed in South Carolina, and as the wife of William Stephenson of Ballymoney is said to have been the sister of John Beatty, elder of the Ballymoney church until he had gone to South Carolina, it is possible that the "call" to the Rev. William Martin was brought on the Hopewell and originated either with John Beatty or with Alexander Brady.

October 1772, carried two items of interest. The first is under the caption of—

TIMOTHY'S MARITIME LIST
Arrived at Charleston

"Oct. 18 Snow, *James and Mary*, John Workman, from Larne."

The second is a news item in the same issue—

"Charleston, Oct. 22. Last Sunday upwards of 200 Irish settlers arrived here in the snow, *James and Mary*, Captain Workman, from Larne. Some other vessels with a greater number on board were soon to follow this."

But almost two months elapsed before the next vessel arrived. Meanwhile what happened to the *James and Mary* passengers is shown by a notice in *The South Carolina Gazette*, Oct. 29, 1772—

"Proclamation by Charles Greville Montagu, Captain General, Governor, [etc.]

"Whereas, the snow *Mary and James*, John Workman, Master, is arrived at the Port of Charles Town from Ireland, with several Passengers who have the Small-Pox on board, now lying off Sullivans Island, I therefore strictly forbid all Persons whatsoever either from going on Board the Snow or Vessel called the Mary and James or near the said Island, at the peril of being prosecuted according to the Laws in that case made and provided, without my express orders and Direction for so doing.

Given . . . etc. . . . this 26th Day of October A.D. 1772
Charles-Greville Montagu"

It was the custom, when passengers were satisfied with their treatment aboard ship to write a letter—for publication —expressing appreciation of the courtesies of the captain, etc., and in the midst of their illness and delays this was not forgotten. The letter was duly published in the *Belfast News Letter* on Tuesday, December 22, 1772, and is of considerable interest. [10]

[10] I am indebted to Mr. Kenneth Darwin, Deputy Keeper of the Public Records of Northern Ireland and Director of the Ulster Scot Historical Society, Belfast, for this letter, as he generously forwarded to me a photo-copy of the page of the paper on which it appeared.

"To the Printers of the Belfast News Letter.

I desire you will insert and continue three times in your Paper, the inclosed Letter, which I received from South Carolina.

Yours,

Larne, 21 Dec. 1772   JAMES McVICKAR.

P. S. My Friend in Charlestown advises me, that they have a great Crop of Rice, but want Ships to carry it to Market.

To Mr. JAMES M'VICKAR, Merchant in Larne.

'SIR,   Charles-Town, Oct. 21, 1772

THESE will inform you, that we arrived here all well and in good spirits the 18th instant (five Children excepted who died in the Passage) after a pleasant and agreeable Passage of seven weeks and one day. — Pleasant with respect to Weather, and agreeable with regard to the Concord and Harmony that subsisted among us all: And, to confirm what we have heard you assert, before we left Ireland, we must say, that we had more than a sufficiency of all kinds of Provisions, and good in their kind: And to speak of Captain Workman, as he justly deserves, we must say with the greatest Truth (and likewise with the greatest Thanks and Gratitude to him) that he treated us all with the greatest Tenderness and Humanity: and seemed even desirous of obliging any one, whom it might be in his Power to serve. If you think proper, we would be desirous you should cause these Things to be inserted in the public News Letter, being sensible they will afford our Friends and Acquaintances great Satisfaction; and we hope they may be of some Use to you and Captain Workman, if you resolve to trade any more in the Passenger Way. Now, in Confirmation of these Things, we subscribe ourselves as follows:

We are, Sir, your Most humble Servants,

Revd Robt. Mc.Clintock,	John Mc.Clintock,	Thos. Makee,
John Peddan,	John Dicky,	James Stinson,
Joseph Lowry,	James Hood,	Wm. Anderson,
Timothy Mc.Clintock,	John Montgomery,	John Thompson,
	John Snody,	Hugh Loggan,
	John Caldwell,	Peter Willey,

Nathan Brown,	Robt. Hadden,	David Thompson,
Samuel Kerr,	Wm. Boyd,	Hugh Mansoad,
James Peddan,	Robt. Machesney,	Robt. Wilson,
Alex. Brown,	Wm. Eashler,	Robt. Ross,
John Brown,	Charles Miller,	John Parker,
Thomas Madill,	John Rickey,	James Young,
Wm. Simpson,	Charles Dunlop,	Robt. Neile.

P. S. We had Sermon every Sabbath, which was great Satisfaction to us. We omitted to let you know, that the Mate, Mr. Bole, as also the common Hands, behaved with great Care and Benevolence towards us."

It should be noted that the surnames of "Robt. McClintock" and "Timothy McClintock" appear in the *Council Journal* as "McLinto," "Robert Hadden" becomes "Robert Hadin," and "Thomas Madill" is "Thomas McDill." These variations indicate the dialect pronunciations used and therefore aid in identifying these passengers in subsequent records.

Charles Dunlop, Hugh Mansoad, James Young, and Robt. Machesney are not included in the list of those persons arriving on this vessel to whom warrants for land were issued. However, Robert's son, Alexander Chesney is listed. This is the Alexander Chesney who was a well-known Loyalist during the Revolution and who ultimately returned to Ireland. From his *Journal* [11] we learn that his father did not apply for free land but instead bought it, thus accounting for his name not appearing on the list. From the same *Journal* we learn a little about the trip. He says that the smallpox had been severe on the vessel and when the surgeon came on board and reported it to the Governor "we were obliged to ride at quarantine first three weeks, and then a second three weeks and 8 days * * * "

"We had a large house during Quarantine allowed for the sick on Sullivans Island which was kept for the purpose of a hospital; one Robinson has a salary from the Government for living there. We went back and forth from hospital to ship for a change. * * * "

[11] E. A. Jones, ed., Journal of Alexander Chesney; A South Carolina Loyalist in the Revolution and after, (Columbus, Ohio, 1921) p. 3.

At length it was over. On 1 December 1772 there is a pertinent entry in the *Council Journal.* [12] This does not specifically identify the petitioners as being those arriving on the *James and Mary* but from other evidence it is clear that they are, as (1) they are the only group from Ireland at that time not otherwise identified, (2) the names of those shown by signatures to the above quoted letter to have come on the *James and Mary* are included in the list of those of the Martin party to whom warrants are directed to be issued (although no ship is named) but did not at that time petition for their land, indicating that the petitions had been presented and the examination taken place previously.

The entry [12] reads—

"The following Persons presented Petitions setting forth that they were Protestants and had lately come to settle in this Province with their Respective Familys from Ireland and were desirous to settle and cultivate some vacant Land in the back parts of the Country. But by Reason of their extreem Poverty they were altogether unable to pay the Fees due to the several offices for their Grants, and that they were in hopes to have received some aid from the Province as their Countrymen had hitherto done, and therefore Prayed his Excellency to Grant them such Relief as in his Goodness he should see fit.

"His Excellency thereupon observed to them that the Bounty given by the Province had ceased long since, and that they had no Reason from Government to expect any such assistance as they Craved. But it appearing that they were very poor, his Excellency proposed to the several officers to deliver out their warrants without expense to them and to take the Risk of being paid by the Public which they severally agreed to —— * * * * the Secretary was ordered to prepare the warrants of survey"

Although the entry states "The following persons" the names of the arrivals on the *James and Mary* are not thereafter listed. The warrants seem to have been prepared under date of 11 December 1772, but not issued. While no record

---

[19] [South Carolina] Council Journal No. 36, Part 2, p. 242.

has been found of instructions to that effect, it appears that the warrants were held for the arrival of the Rev. William Martin, for the names and acres for each are then listed, at the same time as are the warrants for those on the other ships of the Martin party. [13]

At length the other vessels arrived, all within three days.

The *South Carolina Gazette* dated 24 December 1772, reported, among others, the following "Arrivals at Charlestown"——

Dec. 19   Ship Pennsylvania Farmer Charles Robeson Belfast

* * * * *

Dec. 20   Ship Lord Dunluce   James Gillies   Larne

* * * * *

Dec. 22   Ship Hopewell   John Martin   Belfast
          Brigt. Free Mason   John Semple   Newry

In the same issue appeared a news item:

"On Saturday last * * * * *

"The same day arrived the *Pennsylvania Farmer*, Captain Robeson, from Belfast; Sunday, the *Lord Dunluce*, Captain Gillies, from Larne; on Tuesday the *Hopewell*, Captain Martin, from Belfast; and the *Freemason*, Captain Semple, from Newry; all with Irish passengers, above 1000 souls."

The passengers on the *Lord Dunluce* also wrote a letter of commendation for the ship and Captain, which appeared in the *Belfast NewsLetter* 4-8 June 1773. [14]

Charlestown, 15 January 1773.

"For the Belfast News Letter.

We, the undernamed Subscribers, think it is a duty incumbent upon us to acquaint the Publick in general and our Friends in particular, that we went on board from Larne the Ship Lord Dunlace, a stout commodious Vessel, James Gillis, Master; and after eleven Weeks Passage we arrived at Charlestown in South Carolina (our passage being prolonged by contrary Winds, which beat us so far North, and continuing

[13] [South Carolina] Council Journal, vol. 37, p. 23.
[14] From copy published on p. 191 of Ulster Emigration to Colonial America, 1718-1755, by permission of the author and copyright holder Dr. R. J. Dickson.

to blow from the South West, detained us near three Weeks out of our way, notwithstanding all the Care and unwearied Diligence of our Captain, who did not fail to take all safe Advantage, in order to expedite our Way). But the Tediousness of our Voyage was rendered as agreeable to us as possible by the humane treatment of our worthy Captain, and agreeable Company, together with the useful and timely Admonitions of our respected Friend, the Revd. William Martin, who never failed when the Weather and Time would permit, to preach the everlasting gospel to us, the which we esteemed a singular Blessing. We had Plenty of Provisions of good Quality, and so would have had as agreeable a Passage, notwithstanding the Length of it, as any that ever was made from Ireland, had it not happened that the Small-pox broke out in the Vessel, which continued for some Time, and occasioned the Death of some Children; during which Time our Worthy Captain, and the Revd. Mr. Martin were duly employed visiting the Sick, and administering Cordials to their several Necessities, etc. which Disorders would have caused us (according to the Laws of the Land) to have road Quarantine six weeks, had not our Captain, by his Application to a Friend of his, through whose kind Mediation we obtained Liberty to go ashore the Day before the grand Court met, and got the Favour of being called up to get out Warrants before those that had landed before with riding fifteen Days Quarantine, which was a Favour that not many have been favoured with. Again, our worthy Friend Captain Gillis and Mr. Martin did not cease, at the Expiration of our Voyage, to continue their fatherly Care over us, but used their utmost Endeavors to obtain Money to carry us to our Plantations, etc. Therefore we invite all our friends that intend to come to this Land, to sail with Captain Gillis if possible, as he is both a solid, cautious, and careful Captain as ever sailed in the Passenger Way; the which Opinion we were confirmed in by meeting with some Passengers who landed near the same Time, and hearing of their Treatment, concluded that we would rather pay Capt. Gillis something extraordinary, than sail with any other.

John Huey
Samuel Miller
Wm. Fairies
Charles Miller
John Craig
Wm. Humphrey
Archibald McWilliams
James Crawford
John Flemming
Richard Wright
James Sloan
Francis Adams
Wm. Adams
Wm. Miller
Samuel Barber
Hugh Owens
Wm. Greg
John Greg
James Brown
John Agnew
David Montgomery
John Baird
Alexander Fleming
Matthew Fleming
Wm. Crawford
Robert Reed

Abraham Thomson
Robert Hanna
Charles Burnit
John Roarke
John McQuillen
George Cherry
Thomas Weir
David McQuestin
James McQuestin
Wm. Barlow
Samuel Fear
Gilbert Menary
James McLurkin
Richard McLurken
Widow Mebin
Thomas McClurken
James Blair
Brice Blair
Thomas Wilson
David Murray & Family
John McClenaghan
Archibald McNeel
James Wilson
Robert Jameson
John Henring

(The last name appended to this letter does not appear on the list of those applying for land; it may be that this man bought land or it may be that this is the man applying for land as "John Erving." "Gilbert Menary" is "Gilbert McNary," probably "David Murray and Family" is "David Morrow," and "John Huey" is "John Hewie" on the list in the *Council Journal*. [15])

The *Lord Dunluce* with Rev. William Martin aboard arrived on 20 December 1772. As stated in the letter to the Belfast paper, it was quarantined for 15 days only. During this period apparently passengers on all five of the ships had to wait. But promptly thereafter action was taken, as outlined in the next chapter.

---

[15] See Chapter 6 for variations in spelling of surnames.

CHAPTER 4

SETTLEMENT IN SOUTH CAROLINA

I

Getting Their Land

The *Council Journal* for January 6, 1773 states [1]

"The following persons who had lately arrived from Ireland into the Province on the ship *Lord Dunluce* presented petitions for warrants of survey agreeable to their Respective Family Rights, vizt."

followed by the names of the persons and acres of land to which entitled.

A somewhat similar statement is made preceding the list of names of those on the *Hopewell, Pennsylvania Farmer* and *Freemason*. In each case, after the list of names is the statement, "Ordered that the Secretary prepare survey as prayed for by the several petitions."

Between the lists of those coming on the *Pennsylvania Farmer* and the *Freemason* is a list headed "It is ordered by his Excellency the Governor that the Secretary do prepare warrants of survey for the undermentioned persons," without mentioning the ship on which they came or that they have petitioned for land. As the warrants for the persons named in this list are all dated December 11, 1772, at which time the snow *James and Mary* was the only vessel recently arrived from North Ireland ports whose passengers had not already received their warrants and the names of some of the persons on this list to whom warrants were so issued are signed to the letter sent to Ireland by passengers on that vessel and others are known from other sources to have been members of the Rev. William Martin's congregation or to have been passengers on that vessel, it can be definitely stated that the names listed are those who arrived on the snow *James and*

¹ [South Carolina] Council Journal, voL 37, p. 15 et seq.

Mary; that the entry in the *Council Journal* of December 1, 1772, referred to them, that the warrants, dated December 11, had been duly prepared but held for the arrival of the Rev. William Martin and final determination as to the procedure to be followed.

The list of persons on each ship is divided into two groups; one, those who have £5 and so will pay fees for their land, and second, those who have sworn they do not have £5, so are deemed "poor persons" and thus do not have to pay the fees. (In this connection, it may be of interest to note that the fees, as listed in Chapter 1, sec. III, for the cost of the survey would usually amount to from £3 to £5, depending on exactly what was required in the particular case. If Five Pounds was all a family had, in the majority of cases they would have no money left by the time they had their land.)

Extensive research in the "Instructions," statutes, *Council Journal* and other records has failed to discover any authority or reason for the sum of £5 being required. But as only "poor protestants" were entitled to their land free of charge it seems probable it was fixed by administrative decision as the amount which would determine the category into which emigrants from Ireland who petitioned for land would be placed, that is, that a person who arrived in the Colony and did not have as much as £5 would be deemed a "poor protestant."

For names appearing in the *Council Journal* of those to whom warrants were issued and the number of acres to which each were entitled, see sec. III.

It should be rembered that these are not "passenger lists" but lists of those arriving on the respective ships *who applied for free grants of land.* It seems probable that the majority of the passengers *did* apply for free land, even in cases where they had funds and also bought land, as it is known that several did.

Daniel Green Stinson (born 1794, son of William Stinson (Stephenson) who came in the Martin party), writing in the *South Carolina Reporter* at an early date, [2] stated he had in

---

[2] In an article (date unknown) which he furnished to and which was printed in The Reformed Presbyterian (1876).

his possession a letter from Henry and Margaret Malcolm, dated 30 May 1773, County Antrim, Ireland, to their son-in-law, John Lin (who came on the *Lord Dunluce*) in which they mention, "We hear it reported here that Mr. Martin and his Covenanters had ill getting their land and John Cochrane had the occasion of their trouble." (This allusion is not explained. A John Cochrane was a passenger on the *Pennsylvania Farmer* and was granted land on Rocky Creek, Chester Co., but no reference has been found to any "trouble." It would be interesting to know what caused the comment.)

Daniel Green Stinson then went on to say that *he* supposed the trouble was that they had all expected to settle together in a colony, but found lands would not be granted in such a way as to permit it, and they had to scatter. While all were entitled to land, he continues, "Those who had means bought from old settlers." Records indicate, however, that while those with "means" may have bought improved property from earlier settlers, in a number of cases they also took up the free land to which they were entitled and improved it. Nevertheless, it is clear there were those in the group that did not take up any land. For example, Robert Chesney bought his land even before he came (or at least before he left Charlestown) but his young son Alexander took up a grant. Others no doubt did the same.

It is quite understandable that so soon after the Regulator troubles the Governor would not have wanted to see a colony of around 1,000 Irish, who felt they had been forced out of their home in Ireland, settled in one place, and would see to it that they were scattered. There was, however, some freedom of choice, for in many instances it has been noted that the land surveyed for one of the Martin party adjoined land which was already possessed by someone of the same surname; if they could not remain in a group there was a tendency for each to settle where there were relatives.

II

Steps Taken to Collect Data on Each Immigrant

The names listed in the *Council Journal* of those for whom surveys were authorized are those of heads of families (which might consist merely of a single man or woman if such person comprised the family.

The head of a family was entitled to 100 acres for himself and 50 acres for his wife and the same for each other member of his family. [3] In a number of cases adult sons and daughters in a family, who were single, took up land in their own names. (It would be interesting to trace the disposition of the land taken up by young single women, since the condition of receiving a grant was the clearing and improvement of the land.) In some cases it appears that a person did not take up in the beginning all the land to which he was entitled; it has been *assumed* this was because there was not, in the location in which he wished to settle, enough land available, or he may have had some occupation such as weaver, smith, or storekeeper, and only took up enough land for his own family's subsistence. Therefore, the number of acres surveyed for a man does not necessarily indicate the size of his family.

In order to bring together information developed about each immigrant in the Martin party and to avoid much repetition, in Section III of this Chapter instead of giving first the complete extract from the *Council Journal*, then all the surveys found, then any deeds, wills, etc., all data pertaining to one man has been assembled under his name, in sequence and with abbreviations as follows——

(a) First, the entry in the *Council Journal* for January 6, 1773, giving ship by ship introductory statement and name of ship, etc., name of person to whom warrant is to be issued and number of acres to which entitled. (Instead of prefacing this line by "(a)," each individual will be designated by a number, assigned in the sequence in which the name appears in the *Council Journal.*)

(b) Abstract of survey, if identified (see below).

(c) Suggestion as to the county in which, subsequent to 1785, such land was probably located (see below).

(d) Will, deed, or other data which *might* relate to such person (see below).

---

[3] Instructions to Governor Lyttelton, Public Records (South Carolina) vol. XXVI, p. 315 (mss.), in South Carolina Department of Archives and History.

In the abstract of survey mentioned in (b) above——

(1) The following abbreviations are used to identify the records in the South Carolina Department of Archives and History from which data was taken:

P.F. — Plat folder, Pre-Revolutionary plats.

Pl. Bk. — Pre-Revolutionary Plat Book.

Mem. v. — Memorial, volume.

(2) Data is given in the following sequence:

Number of Plat folder or Book;

Date of precept or warrant (i.e., authorization of survey);

Number of acres surveyed or laid out;

Description;

Names of persons whose land adjoined tract being surveyed (abbreviated as "Bd'd.")

Date of survey or of certificate of survey.

With reference to (c), the county in which located: If a stream or other physical feature indicated in the survey is one of which the location is known or has an unusual name so could be identified with reasonable degree of accuracy, the county into which a landmark of that name subsequently fell, when counties were established, is indicated. In many instances there are numerous streams of the same name or one traverses several counties. In such case the various possibilities are indicated. For positive identification, deeds and wills, in the counties suggested, of persons of the name of the person for whom the land was surveyed and those shown as adjoining owners will need to be consulted. It has been noticed that within a short time after settlement there were a number of instances in which the land taken up was sold and land bought in another county. Particularly noticeable was the shift from what is now Spartanburg and York to what is now Chester and Fairfield. Reasons may have been the proximity of Indians in the first named, or desire to be nearer their minister and church.

As for the deeds, wills, or other documents cited or abstracted which are in some instances included under (d) —

it must be emphasized that such additional data is NOT based on an absolute identification of the person making such will or deed with the immigrant whose name appeared above; it is a *probable* identification which may be readily checked by further search in the records of the county indicated. Such citation or abstract is used to demonstrate the procedure to be followed by utilizing one record to indicate another record and so on, in order to trace the connection and so to identify the known ancestor with an immigrant or conversely. Positive identification was made in a few cases in order to demonstrate it is practicable to determine whether the immigrant settled on the tract surveyed for him or sold it. If he settled there, often he can be traced further by subsequent records until it can be proven whether he is or is not the progenitor of a latter known ancestor. If he sold it soon, frequently his new place of residence at that time can thereby be discovered and records there utilized in the same way.

III

"In the Council Chamber, Wednesday the 6th January 1773" [4]

* * * * * *

The following persons who had lately arrived from Ireland into this province in the ship *Lord Dunluce* presented petitions for warrants of Survey agreeable to their Respective Family Rights, vizt——

In South Carolina	*Acres*
1. REV'D WILLIAM MARTIN	400

(b) P.F. 1264; 6 Jan. 1773; 400 acres, Craven Co., on waters of Fishing Creek; bd'd Mary Gaston, John Gaston, Elesabeth Strong; 8 March 1773.

(c) Chester.

(d) See Chapter 2 for further account of Rev. William Martin.

2. JAMES M'LURKAM	300

(b) P.F. 1226; 6 Jan. 1773; 350 acres in Craven Co., on Durbins Creek branch called Bowen Branch; sur. 3 Feb. 1773.

(c) Laurens or Greenville (but see Chester).

(d) Chester Co. Will Bk. 1, p. 110: James McClurken, 9 Dec. 1794; pr. Sept. 1795; sons, Thomas and Sam; daughters, Eleanor, Jean, Cath-

---

[4] [South Carolina] Council Journal, No. 37, pp. 15-25 inc.

erine, Jenet, Lillys; James' children; John's sons Andrew and James; Samuel's son James; Dau. Catherine's son James Boyd; Dau. Jean's son James Waid; Dau. Jenet's son James McClurken; Dau. Eleander's dau. Mary Young. Ex.: Sons-in-law John Maben and David Waid.

3. ROBERT JAMIESON 250

(b) Pl. Bk. vol. 19, p. 489; 6 Jan. 1773; in Craven Co. on waters of Rocky Creek; bd'd Robert Coulter, John Casky, Thomas Huston, David Grimbs, Mary Coulter, vacant land; cer. 6 June 1774. Ord. Co. 3 April 1775 for Thomas Singleton.

(c) Chester.

4. ANDREW AGNEW 300

(b) P.F. 13; 6 Jan. 1773; laid out to John Agnew (earlier first name erased and "John" substituted); in Craven Co. on south fork of Wateree Creek; bd'd Nicolas Thompson, vacant land; sur. 24 Feb. 1773.

5. DAVID MONTGOMERY 350

(b) P.F. 1337; 6 Jan. 1773; in Craven Co. on branch of Wateree Creek called Horse Branch; bd'd John Agnew, Moses Hollis; sur. 8 March 1773.

(c) York, Lancaster, Chester or Fairfield.

(d) See Fairfield Co., Wills 1, Bk. 5, p. 78.

6. JAMES BROWN 350

(b) P.F. 209; 6 Jan. 1773, Craven Co.; Waters of Kings and Connors Creek; bd'd Frances Wilson, James Neal, David Tennant, vacant land; sur. 25 Feb. 1773; Dd. 9 Aug. 1774.

(c) Newberry.

(d) See Laurens Co. Will Bk. 1-E-96 (?).

7. JOHN HEWIE 150

(b) P.F. 844; 6 Jan. 1773; in Craven Co. on branch of Pacolet; bd'd Joseph French, Zack Bullock; sur. 10 May 1773.

(c) Spartanburg, Union.

8. JOHN RORK 100

9. WILLIAM STORMONT 150

10. JOHN McCHANTS 100

(b) Probably P.F. 1159; 6 Jan. 1773; laid out to "John McCants" 100 acres in Craven Co., waters of 25-mile Creek; sur. 11 Feb. 1773.

(c) Kershaw.

(d) Fairfield Co. Will Bk. 1-6, p. 25. John McCance — 14 Jan. 1813: Wife Sarah; sons, Robert, Samuel, John, William, Jim; daughters, Amy, Sarah, Liliah; children under age: Alexander, George, Jeremiah, Andr', Mary, Margaret, Rosey. (But see Nos. 88 and 204)

11. FRANCIS ADAMS 350
   (b) P.F. 7; Jan. 1773; in Craven Co., on branches of Rum Creek; bd'd James McHughes, vacant land; cer. 16 March 1773.
   (c) York.
   (d) Possibly testator or father of testator: York Co. Wills, vol. 2, p. 170; Francis Adams, 2 Sept. 1824, pr. 20 July 1825; Dau. Martha Byers; sons, William, Francis, John (if he comes to this country). Ex., one was Williamson Byers.

12. MARY ADAMS 100
   (b) P.F. 8; 6 Jan. 1773; on branches of Dry Creek, waters of Cawtaba, near McDaniel's land; bd'd all sides vacant land.
   (c) Lancaster.

13. HUGH OWEN 100
   (b) Pl. Bk. 19, p. 26, and Memorials, vol. 12, p. 393; 200 acres to Elizabeth Henry; in Craven Co., St. Marks Parish, at head branch of Sawneys Creek; bd'd Wm. Sanders, Eva Catherine Hoafman, Stephen Miller; by order of Council 4 May 1773 100 acres of above survey granted 5 May 1773 to Hugh Owens, original right of Elizabeth Henley having lapsed.
   (c) Kershaw.

14. JOHN OWEN 100
   (b) P.F. 1449; 6 Jan. 1773; in Granville Co., waters of Salt Catcher on Jackson's branch; bd'd Andrew Sayer, Thomas Baker, Sr.; 10 April 1775.
   (c) Barnwell, Edgefield.

15. SAMUEL FEAR 250
   (b) P.F. 567; 6 Jan. 1773; in Craven Co., north side of Saluda River on a draft of Bush River. Bd'd John Rankin, Thomas Hopkins, Robt. Mills, Henry Delmar. Sur. 30 Jan. 1773.
   (c) Newberry.
   (d) Newberry Will Bk. 1-C, p. 18; Samuel Fear, 6 Sept. 1776; 28 July 1800. To son Samuel, John Cots land; 100 acres to son William, 100 to daughter Margret; other 50 to wife. Ex.: John Barlo and William McClelland. Wit.: John Barlow, John McClelland.

16. JOHN FLEMING 150
   (b) P.F. 592; 6 Jan. 1773; in Craven Co. on branch of Wateree River called Bull Run; bd'd William McCaw, Wm. Coulterd. Sur. 30 Jan. 1773.
   (c) Chester.
   (d) Chester Wills, vol. 1-A-43: John Fleeman of Bull Run on waters of Rocky Creek, 28 July 1780, 2 July 1798; wife Elizabeth, for life; then to Samuel, son of John Burns (on stated conditions); if not met to be sold and proceeds given to Church of Covenanted Dissent under care of Reformed Presbytery; Hugh McWilliams, Jas. McQuestion and John

Kell to have care, etc. To brother John McCoune and sister Anne McCoune; to nephews Alex. McCoune and John McCoune, Jr.; to nieces Nancy Caldwell and Mary McDoal; to brother Robert Cowan and sister Jane Cowan and their children John, Alexander and Elizabeth. Exs.: James McQuestine and John Kell; Hugh McMillen if John Kell dies. Wit. Ofadam Edgar, William Edgar.

17. JOHN CRAIG 350

(b) P.F. 378; 6 Jan. 1773; in Craven Co., on waters of Linches Creek; bd'd on north by Province line; sur. 25 May 1773.

(c) Lancaster, Chesterfield.

18. JOHN GREG 150

(b) P.F. 745; 6 Jan. 1773; in 96 Dist., north side of Tyger River on waters of Cane Creek; bd'd George Strawn, John McLelan; sur. 31 May 1773.

(c) Union.

19. JOHN CAMBLE 300

(b) P.F. 273; 6 Jan. 1773; laid out for John Campbell in Craven Co. on Rocky Creek; bd'd James Turner, John Biggams land, Wm. McGarely, Jas. Harper. Sur. 23 Jan. 1773.

(c) Chester.

(d) Possibly Chester Co. Will Bk., vol. 2 (Bk. H), p. 8; John Campbell; proved 21 Oct. 1817; names wife Mary; sons James, Samuel, Major, John, Alexander, William, Joseph; daughter Mary.

20. ROBERT WILSON 250

(b) P.F. 2035; 6 Jan. 1773, in Craven Co., on waters of Little River; sur. 16 Feb. 1773.

(c) Abbeville, Chester, Fairfield, Richland, Laurens, Newberry.

21. GILBERT M'NARY 250

(b) P.F. 1232; 6 Jan. 1773, in Craven Co., N. W. side of Duncans Creek on Cold Beards fork; bd'd William Harris. Sur. 11 Feb. 1773.

(c) Laurens.

22. JANE GREG 100

(b) Pl. Bk., vol. 16, p. 224; 6 Jan. 1773; laid out for Jean Gregg on south branch of Little River; bd'd Samuel Minn, Samuel Mabrly; sur. 3 Feb. 1773.

(c) Chester, Fairfield, Richland.

23. GEORGE CHERRY 100

(b) P.F. 322; 6 Jan. 1773; in Craven Co., waters of Fishing Creek; bd'd vacant land.

(c) Chester.

(d) Chester Co. Deed Bk. M, p. 209; 25 Sept. 1809, George Cherry sells 100 acres, on waters of Fishing Creek, to Benj. Booth. Janet, wife of George waived dower. (Other Cherry records in Chester Co.)

24. JOHN MORTANT 100

(b) Pl. Bk., vol. 18, p. 559; 6 Jan. 1773; in Craven Co. on branch of Rocky Creek; bd'd Peter Wilie, Robert Walker, John Walker; vacant land; cert. 22 Jan. 1773.

(c) Chester.

(d) Chester Co. Will Bk. 1-2D-6; John Morton, 25 May 1799, 2 May 1806; wife Elizabeth; daughter Martha's children; grandson John Morton McCaw, granddaughter Jenny; son-in-law James McCaw. Ex.: James Wylie, William Kenny. Wit. Edward McDaniel, Samuel McCaw, William McCaw.

25. HUGH DOUGLAS 100

(b) P.F. 479; 6 Jan. 1773; in Granville Co., bd'd Kirland, Keabler,. and Turkey Creek (partly destroyed; only plat and endorsement left); sur. 3 Feb. 1773.

(c) Orangeburg, Lexington.

26. JOHN FLEMING 300

(b) P.F. 592; 6 Jan. 1773; in Craven Co. on head of Black River; bd'd Samuel Crismas; sur. 7 May 1773.

(c) Sumter, Kershaw.

27. ARCH'D MCWILLIAM 250

(b) Pl. Bk., vol. 18, p. 345; 6 Jan. 1773, in Ninety-Six Dist., between Broad and Saluda Rivers on a branch of Little River; bd'd Thomas Jones, Mrs. Williamson, John Rodgers, Mr. Wodert.

(c) Laurens, Newberry.

28. JAMES BLAIR 250

(b) Possibly P.F. 135; 6 Jan. 1773; 230 acres in Craven Co., on drafts of Fishing Creek; bd'd James Ferguson, Thos. Martain, Wm. McFadden, James Ferguson, Sr., Robt. McFadden; sur. 16 Feb. 1773. (But see No. 331, James Blair, on Pennsylvania Farmer.)

(c) Chester.

(d) Chester Co. Wills, vol. 1 (Bk. E, p. 172), p. 30: James Blair, 14 Sept. 1796, pr. August 1812; wife, Margaret; sons: James, William; daughters: Martha, Sarah; son-in-law, R. Wyte.

29. HENRY REA 250

(b) P.F. 1572; 6 Jan. 1773; 150 acres, as part of 250 acres, on Thickety Creek, Craven Co.; bd'd Alexander, James Kenaday, John Gilmore, David Hopkins, Zacaria Bell; sur. 8 June 1773. Also 95 acres being part of balance of 250 acres in Warrant, on Hays branch, south side Wateree River, Craven Co.; bd'd Dr. Street, Edman Strange, Samnel Land, William Land. Sur. 8 June 1773.

(c) Richland.

30. JAMES TWEED 100

 (b) There were two men of this name on the Lord Dunluce. Only one survey or grant has been located.

P.F. 1905; 6 Jan. 1773; in Craven Co., on northeast side of Reyburne Creek on small branch called Lick Creek; cert. 21 March 1773. NOTE: This survey may be either for the above James Tweed (No. 30) or for James Tweed below (No. 140), which see.

 (c) Laurens.

31. ADAM MCRORY 150

 (b) Pl. Bk., vol. 18, p. 340; 6 Jan. 1773; on waters of Little River in Craven Co.; bd'd Samuel Cleg, James McDowell, Wm. Boyd; cert. Dec. 22, 1773.

 (c) Fairfield.

32. JOHN ERVING 150

33. JOHN MCLENAN 350

 (b) P.F. 1226; 6 Jan. 1773; 220 acres in Craven Co. Northeast side of Reyburne Creek called Bradshaws Branch; bd'd Capt. James Lindly, Philip Sherrel, John Owings, Alex'r Carmack, David Rea. Sur. 10 Feb. 1773.

 (c) Laurens, Abbeville.

 (d) See Abbeville Wills, Bk. 3, p. 453.

34. WILLIAM MCMURTY 100

35. MARY LIDEY 100

36. WILLIAM MOORE 100

37. THOS. MCCLURKEN 100

 (b) P.F. 1169; 6 Jan. 1773; 100 acres to Thomas McClarkan; in 96 Dist. on north side of Reyburnes Creek; bd'd Robert Box; sur. 24 March 1773.

 (c) Laurens.

 (d) See Laurens Co. Will Bk. 2-F-129.

38. JAMES MCLURKAM 100

 (b) P.F. 1109; 6 Jan. 1773; 100 acres to James McClurkam, in Craven Co., south side Enoree River; bd'd Mordacai Moore; sur. 27 Feb. 1773.

 (c) Laurens.

39. SAMUEL MCLURKAM 100

 (b) P.F. 1169; 6 Jan. 1773; to Samuel McClurkam; in 96 Dist., waters of Raeburn Creek; bd'd James Williams, Thomas McClurkam; sur. 20 March 1773.

 (c) Laurens.

40. MARY McLURKAM 100

(b) P.F. 1169; 6 Jan. 1773; to Mary McClurkam; in Craven Co., northeast side of Reyburn Creek, on Lick Br.; bd'd William Williamson, Esq., Thomas Weir, Jr.; James Tweed; sur. 20 March 1773.

(c) Laurens.

41. ELANOR McLURKAM 100

(b) P.F. 1169; 6 Jan. 1773; to Eleanor McClurkam; in Craven Co., northwest Durbins Creek branch called Bowens Branch; bd'd James McClurkam, Patrick Cunningham; sur. 18 March 1773.

(c) Laurens.

42. LILLIAS McLURKAM 100

(b) P.F. 1169; 6 Jan. 1773; to Lillias McClurkam; in Craven Co., 96 District, branch of Enoree River called Beaver Dam Branch; sur. 23 March 1773.

(c) Laurens.

43. JANE McLURKAM 100

(b) P.F. 1169; 6 Jan. 1773; to Jane McClurkam; in Craven Co., waters of Reaburn Creek; sur. 13 April 1773.

(c) Laurens.

44. THOMAS WILSON 300

(b) P.F. 2036; 6 Jan. 1773; in Colleton Co., on branch of north fork of Long Cane called Jonston Creek; bd'd John Hunter, William McCalaster, John Jonston, Job Smith; sur. 23 May 1774.

(c) Abbeville.

45. HUGH MONTGOMERY 100

(b) P.F. 1369; 6 Jan. 1773; in Craven Co. on waters of Little River; bd'd John Smith; sur. 16 March 1773.

(c) Fairfield.

(d) Fairfield Wills, vol. 1, Bk. 5, p. 80. Hugh Montgomery, Sr., 10 March 1804, pr. 7 May 1804; wife Margaret; children: David, Charles, Margaret, Elizabeth, Martha, Hugh, Jane.

46. ROBERT READ 150

(b) P.F. 1576; 6 Jan. 1773; in Craven Co. on Branch of Rocky Creek, waters of Wateree River; bd'd James Stewart, Joshua Perrey, Alexd'r Miller; sur. 8 May 1773.

(c) Chester.

47. JANET SMITH 100

(b) P.F. 1747; 6 Jan. 1773; in Craven Co., south side of Enoree, waters of Indian Creek; bd'd Richard Brooks, William Largan, Thos. Garret, Clement Gore; sur. 21 Jan. 1773.

(c) Newberry, Laurens.

48. WILLIAM DIAL 100

(b) P.F. 454; 6 Jan. 1773; in Craven Co., on south side of Broad River, branch of Kings Creek; bd'd James Wilson, Elizabeth Brown.

(c) Newberry, Laurens.

(d) See Laurens Co. Will Bk. 1-E-140.

49. MARGARET DIAL 100

(b) P.F. 454; 6 Jan. 1773; in Craven Co., waters of King Creek, south side Enoree River; bd'd John Willson, Elizabeth Brown, William Dial, John McCullough; sur. 5 Feb. 1773.

(c) Newberry, Laurens.

(d) See Laurens Co. Will Bk. 1-c-1-114.

50. JOHN MCCULLOCH 100

(b) P.F. 1180; 6 Jan. 1773; in Craven Co., south side Enoree River, on branch called Kings Creek; bd'd Jean Willson, Margaret Dial, John Brown, Samuel Gilston; sur. 1 March 1773.

(c) Newberry, Abbeville.

(d) See Abbeville Co. Wills, vol. 2, p. 33.

51. SARAH CRELLMAN 100

(b) P.F. 387; 6 Jan. 1773; Barkeley Co., in fork between Broad River and Saluda, on branch of Indian Creek called Hendrick's Creek, waters of Enoree River; bd'd Michael Mince, James Beard, Will'm Neibours; sur. 8 April 1773.

(c) Laurens, Newberry.

52. CHARLES MILLER 200

(b) P.F. 1301; 6 Jan. 1773; in Barkley Co., in fork between Broad River and Saluda, southwest side of Enoree River; bd'd river, James Townsend, James Willson; sur. 12 Feb. 1773.

(c) Laurens, Newberry.

53. WILLIAM HUMPHREY 100

54. DAVID MCQUESTION 400

(b) Pl. Bk. vol. 18, p. 337; 6 Jan. 1773; to David McQuistion; in Craven Co. on small branch of Rocky Creek; bd'd by Wm. Martin, James Burns, John Henderson, John Mills, vacant land; cert. 12 Feb. 1773.

(c) Chester.

(d) (See National Genealogical Society Quarterly, June 1944, p. 44.)

55. JAMES MCQUESTION 400

(b) Pl. Bk. vol. 18, p. 334; 6 Jan. 1773; to James McQuiston; in Craven Co., branch of Rocky Creek; bd'd John Fleming, Mary Couter, John Knox, Robert and John Walker; vacant land; cert. 7 June 1773.

(c) Chester.

56. WILLIAM FAIRY 200

(b) P.F. 559; 6 Jan. 1773; in Craven Co., bd'd William Boyd, David Chesnut, John Pike, Matthew Grimbs, Elisha Garets; sur. 2 Feb. 1773.

(c) Chester, York.

(d) York Co. Will Index, David Faries; in York Co. Wills, vol. 1, p. 367; David Farris, 18 April 1805, pr. 15 Nov. 1805; wife Nancy; sons, David, John (now absent in the Western Country), James (if he lives to maturity), Joshua, Isaac; daughters Margaret Farris, Mary Farris, Sarah Farris (under age).

57. THOMAS CREIGHTON 100

(b) P.F. 386; 6 Jan. 1773; on branches of Granas Quarter, Parish of St. Marks, Craven Co.; bd'd Mr. Kashaw's land, Judith Brown; sur. 15 Feb. 1773.

(c) Kershaw.

58. THOMAS CREIGHTON, JR. 100

(b) P.F. 386; 6 Jan. 1773; Craven Co. on small branch of Little Lynches Creek; sur. 28 Jan. 1773.

(c) Kershaw, Lancaster.

59. THOMAS BOGGS 100

(b) P.F. 146; 6 Jan. 1773; to Thomas Bogs; on Peoples Creek, branch of Broad River near the Cherokee Ford thereof, in 96 Dist.; bd'd vacant land; cert. 26 March 1773.

(c) Spartanburg.

60. SAMUEL MILLER 100

(b) P.F. 1308; 6 Jan. 1773; in Craven Co. on north side of Santee; bd'd by Francis Green, John Chisholm; sur. 3 June 1773.

(c) Kershaw.

(d) See Kershaw Co. Will Bk. 1-A-1-2.

61. ROBERT WALKER (sic) 100

(b) Possibly P.F. 1939; 2 March 1773, on waters of Rocky Creek in Craven Co.; bd'd Philip Walker, William Harper; sur. 6 March 1773.

(c) Chester.

(d) Chester Co. Wills, vol. 1, p. 79; 19 Dec. 1792, pr. 14 Aug. 1793. Daughters: Esther, Jain, Johanna; sons: Alexander, Robert (under age); sons-in-law: Abraham Gill, John Cooper; wit.: E. H. H. Walker, Thomas Blair, Pelikah (?) Walker.

62. JOHN McQUILLION 200

(b) Pl. Bk. 18, p. 338; Craven Co. in Camden Dist., on waters of 25-mile creek; bd'd John Wilson, James Randel, vacant land; sur. 8 Mar. 1773.

(c) Kershaw, Richland.

63. MARY McQUILLON 100

(b) Pl. Bk. 18; 6 Jan. 1773; to Mary McQuillion, in Barkley Co., in

Orangeburgh Dist., on a branch of four holes; Infringer's land, lands unknown, and vacant land; sur. 27 Jan. 1773.

(c) Orangeburg, Berkeley, Dorchester.

64. MARTHA McQUILLON 100

(b) Pl. Bk. 18, 6 Jan. 1773; in Barkley Co., in Orangeburg Dist., on Paul Branch, the waters of four holes; bd'd vacant land; sur. 10 April 1773.

(c) Orangeburg, Berkeley, Dorchester.

65. JANET McWILLIAM 100

(b) P.F. 1237; 6 Jan. 1773; in 96 Dist. between Broad and Saluda Rivers, on branch of Dunkens Creek; bd'd Noland McCurly; sur. 19 Feb. 1773.

(c) Laurens.

66. AGNES ALLEN 100

(b) P.F. 20; 6 Jan. 1773; in Craven Co. on branch of Warriors Creek, waters of Annaree River, between Broad and Saluda Rivers; bd'd William Young, vacant land; sur. 15 Feb. 1773.

(c) Laurens.

67. JAMES CRAWFORD 200

(b) P.F. 382; 6 Jan. 1773; in 96 Dist. on north side of South Fork of Pacolet River; bd'd vacant land; sur. 5 June 1773.

(c) Spartanburg, Union.

68. WILLIAM CRAWFORD 200

(b) P.F. 384; 6 Jan. 1773; in Craven Co., on branch of Wateree Creek; bd'd John McGuirts, Samuel Boyakin; sur. 30 March 1773.

(c) York.

(d) Possibly testator in York Will Bk. 1-516; 16 Aug. 1813, pr. 4 Oct. 1813. William Crawford; wife Mary; sons: James, William; daughters: Agnes (single), Mary, Margaret, representatives of dau. Isabella.

69. ALEX'R FLEMING 400

70. WILLIAM MILLER 200

(b) P.F. 1310; 6 Jan. 1773; to William Miller, Sen'r.;[5] in Craven Co. on north side of Santee on branch of Gills Creek called 8-mile Branch; bd'd Thomas Miller; sur. 19 Feb. 1773.

(c) Richland, Kershaw.

71. THOMAS MILLER 100

(b) P.F. 1309; 6 Jan. 1773; in Craven Co., north side of Santee River on branch of Gills Creek called 8-mile Branch; bd'd William Miller, Sr., William Miller, Jr.; sur. 19 Feb. 1773.

---

[5] It should be remembered that at that time "Senior" and "Junior" did not indicate father and son, but merely an older and younger man in the same locality.

(c) Richland.

72. WILLIAM MILLER 100

(b) P.F. 1311; 6 Jan. 1773; to William Miller, Jun'r.; on north side of Santee on branch of Gills Creek called Eight-mile Branch; bd'd Thomas Miller; sur. 19 Feb. 1773.

(c) Richland.

73. ROBERT HANNAH 100

(b) Pl. Bk. 15, p. 283; 6 Jan. 1773; to Robert Hannah, Sen'r.; in Craven Co., south side Broad River, waters of Cannan Creek, bd'd Samuel Chapman, ——— Timberman, William McLelland, Thomas Shaw; sur. 29 Jan. 1773.

(c) Newberry, Lexington.

74. ROBERT HANNAH 100

(b) P.F. 786; 6 Jan. 1773; to Robert Hannah, junior; in Craven Co. on waters of Cane Creek; bd'd Hamilton Murdock, Agnes Allen; sur. 15 Feb. 1773.

(c) Lancaster, Laurens.

75. CHARLES BUTNETT 200

(b) P.F. 257; 6 Jan. 1773; in Craven Co., south side of Broad River on Cannan Creek; bd'd Samuel Chapman, J. Chapman, bounty land, Abraham Thomson, Moses Kirklin; sur. 18 Jan. 1773.

(c) Newberry, Lexington.

76. ABRAHAM THOMSON 300

(b) P.F. 1864; 6 Jan. 1773; in Craven Co., south side of Broad River waters of Cannan Creek; bd'd Thomas Shaw, William and John Barlow, Samuel Chapman, Charles Butnet, Moses Kirkelin; sur. 18 Jan. 1773.

(c) Newberry, Lexington.

77. WILLIAM THOMSON 100

(b) P.F. 1872; 6 Jan. 1773; 43 acres in Berkeley Co. on waters of Bush Creek; bd'd Robert Mills, William Mills, Isreal Gaunt, Timothy Thomas, Samuel Fares; sur. 24 Feb. 1773.

Also P.F. 1872; 6 Jan. 1773; 25 acres in Berkeley Co. on waters of Bush Creek; bd'd George Hartle, James Yeldall, William Mills, Robert Mills; sur. 24 Feb. 1773.

(c) Laurens.

78. MARY THOMSON 100

(b) P.F. 1869; 6 Jan. 1773; in Berkeley Co. on small branch of Bush Creek; bd'd John Scott, Jeremiah Ham; sur. 26 May 1773.

(c) Laurens.

79. PATRICK MCMICHAEL 150

(b) P.F. 1229; 6 Jan. 1773; in Craven Co., north side Saluda River, waters of Bush River; bd'd John Edwards, John Regan, Owen Debit, William McLelland, Rose McLelland; sur. 30 Jan. 1773.

(c) Laurens, Newberry.

80. GRIZELL MAYBEAN 200

(b) P.F. 1274; 6 Jan. 1773; in Craven Co., branch of Rocky Creek; bd'd Francis Adams, Daniel Cotney, Thomas Burns, Col. Middleton; sur. 22 Jan. 1773.

(c) Chester.

(d) Chester Co. Deed Book N, p. 337; William Steenson of Chester Co., planter, to John Stinson of same, planter, 12 Sept. 1806, 62 acres and 1/2 mill there, part of 200 acres on waters of Rocky Creek granted Grisle Maben.

81. HENRY MAYBEAN 100

(b) P.F. 1274; 6 Jan. 1773, in 96 District, south side of north fork of Pacolet River; bd'd James Hamilton; sur. 3 June 1773.

(c) Spartanburg.

82. JOHN MAYBEAN 100

(b) P.F. 1274; 6 Jan. 1773; in Camden Dist.; both sides Bullocks Creek; bd'd Wm. Dunlap, John Givens, Gilbert Watson; sur. 29 March 1773.

(c) York.

83. THOMAS MAYBEAN 100

(b) P.F. 1274; 6 Jan. 1773; in 96 Dist. on south side of North Fork of Pacolet River; bd'd Henry Maybean; 4 June 1773.

(c) Spartanburg.

84. ELIZABETH MAYBEAN 100

(b) P.F. 1274; 6 Jan. 1773; in Craven Co. on south fork of Rocky Creek; bd'd William Stanford, Nickalas Thompson, Buckner Haigwood; sur. 9 Feb. 1773.

(c) Chester.

85. SAMUEL IRVINE 150

(b) P.F. 939; 6 Jan. 1773; to Samuel Irving; in Craven Co.; bd'd William Archer, Wm. Stanford, Col. Middleton; sur. 6 Feb. 1773.

(c) Chester.

86. CHRISTOPHER STRONG 300

(b) P.F. 1810; 5 Jan. 1773; in Craven Co., on waters of Rocky Creek; bd'd Henry Isbel, Widow Dunseeth (?); sur. 5 May 1773.

(c) Chester

(d) Chester Co. Deed Bk. E, p. 123; Christopher Strong, weaver, sells to Samuel Erwin, weaver, 16 Sept. 1791, land described in survey, refers to Grant Bk. xxx, p. 144, and Memorial M. No. 14, p. 121.

87. PRICE BLAIR 100

88. ELIZABETH McCHANTS 100

(b) P.F. 1158; 6 Jan. 1773; to Elizabeth McCants; in Craven Co. on branch of Sedar Creek; sur. 11 Feb. 1773.

(c) Lancaster, Richland, Fairfield.

(d) Possibly Fairfield Will Bk. 1-6-25; 1-7-49.

89. ROBERT HOVE 250

(b) Probably Pl. Bk., vol. 15, p. 354; 6 April 1773; to Robert Haure (or Hauve), 300 acres in Craven Co., north side Black Mungo Creek, on branch known as Muddy Creek; bd'd James Cains, George King, vacant land; sur. 20 May 1773.

(c) Williamsburg.

90. DAVID MORROW 450

(b) P.F. 1361; 6 Jan. 1773; in Craven Co. on waters of Sandy River; bd'd vacant land; sur. 7 Feb. 1773.

(c) Chester.

91. ELIZABETH MORROW 100

(b) P.F. 1361; 6 Jan. 1773; in Craven Co., on head of Sandy River; bd'd Joseph McCinley, Paul Ferguson, Samuel Woodsides, vacant land; sur. 6 Feb. 1773.

(c) Chester.

92. SAMUEL BARBER 200

(b) P.F. 73; 6 Jan. 1773; on waters of Rocky Creek and south side of said creek in Craven Co.; bd'd Hugh Wilson, Col. Middleton, vacant land.

(c) Chester.

93. JAMES BARBER 100

(b) P.F. 73; 6 Jan. 1773; in Craven Co.; bd'd Wm. Stroud, Thomas Morris, John Dies, Joseph Tilford; sur. 11 Feb. 1773.

(c) Chester.

94. ISABEL BARBER 100

(b) P.F. 73; 6 Jan. 1773; in Craven Co. on Cedar Creek; bd'd Joseph Kershaw, Thomas Starks, James Kershaw; sur. 1 May 1773.

(c) Chesterfield, Richland, Lancaster, Fairfield.

95. JOSEPH BARBER 200

(b) P.F. 73; 6 Jan. 1773; on south branch of Little Linches Creek in Craven Co.; bd'd vacant land.

(c) Lancaster, Kershaw.

96. JOHN BEARD 300

(b) P.F. 1; 5 Jan. 1773; on branch of Indian Creek, waters of Enoree; bd'd Alexander Dunlap, Hugh Read, Samuel Kelly, Harman Davis, Jonah Reeder, William Young; sur. 2 March 1773.

(c) Newberry.

(d) Newberry Co. Wills, vol.. 1, Bk. D, p. 29; John Beard, Nov. 1798, pr. 5 Nov. 1804. Wife Elizabeth; daughters: Agnes Gordon (and her daughter Jane when of age), Jennet Richey, Jane Montgomery (and her daughter Jane when of age) Elenar if she comes of age; grandson John Beard Richey; Margaret Campbell.

97. JOHN ADAMS 100

(b) P.F. 8; 6 Jan. 1773; on Hannahs Creek, branch of Gils Creek, Waxhaw Settlement; bd'd Capt. John Barkley's land; John Belk, vacant land; sur. 7 March 1773 to Patrick Cain.

(c) Lancaster.

98. RACHEL ADAMS 100

(b) P.F. 9; 6 Jan. 1773; on Hannahs Creek, branch of Gils Creek, Waxhaw Settlement; bd'd by Anguish Black, Isaac Bass, Edmund Hull; sur. 6 March 1773 for Patrick Cain.

(c) Lancaster.

(d) Memorials, vol. 13, p. 230. Tract described above, deed delivered 15 February 1775 to William Adams.

99. AGNES MCKENLEY 100

(b) Pl. Bk. vol. 18, p. 275; 6 Jan. 1773; to Agnes McKinly; on Singletons Creek; bd'd ——— Clanton, vacant; cert. 20 May 1773.

(c) Kershaw.

100. WILLIAM ADAMS 150

(b) P.F. 10; 6 Jan. 1773; on head of Lambs branch, waters of Wateree River; bd'd vacant land.

(c) Kershaw, York.

101. WILLIAM MILLER 150

(b) P.F. 1310; 6 Jan. 1773; in Craven Co., on the Hanging Rock branch; bd'd Mark Cole; John Aleby; sur. 4 March 1773.

(c) Lancaster, Kershaw.

102. ELIZ'TH JOHNSTON 100

(b) P.F. 965; 6 Jan. 1773; on Turkey Quarter, branch of Barkley Creek, Waxhaw Settlement; Craven Co.; sur. 6 March 1773. "Pet. for by Wm. Adams."

(c) Lancaster.

103. JAMES MCCLURE 100

104. JOHN WILSON 100

(b) P.F. 2032; 6 Jan. 1773; in Craven Co.; Canes, bd'd north side by Broad River; sur. 25 March 1773.

105. JOHN HINDMAN 100

(b) Pl. Bk. vol. 17, p. 10; 8 Jan. 1773; in Craven Co., on Londonbridge

Creek, on south side of Broad River; bd'd Francis Wilkey, vacant land; sur. 15 March 1773.

106. ROBERT BRADFORD 350

(b) P.F. 174; 6 Jan. 1773; 206 acres in Craven Co. on branch of Turkey Creek; bd'd Joseph Gladney, Davidson's corner, John Ross, Michael McGarity; sur. 12 Feb. 1773.

(c) Chester, York.

(d) **Probable testator:** Chester Co. Wills, vol. 1, Bk. A, p. 39; Robert Bradford, 5 Dec. 1785, pr. ———— 1785; wife, son John; son-in-law John Ball; children, William, Robert, James, David, Andrew, Mary.

107. JOHN SCOTT 300

(b) P.F. 1677; 6 Jan. 1773; in Craven Co., on west side of Turkey Creek; bd'd James Cambel, Robert Cowin, Joseph Alexander, John Gilmore; sur. 22 March 1773.

(c) Chester, York.

108. WILLIAM SCOTT 100

(b) P.F. 1680; 6 Jan. 1773; to William Scoat; in Craven Co. on branch of Turkey Creek; bd'd Robert Cowan, John Scoat, Joseph Alexander; sur. 25 June 1774.

(c) Chester, York.

109. JAMES SLOAN 250

(b) P.F. 1738; 6 Jan. 1773; in Craven Co., waters of Tiger River; bd'd John McCrary, John Raymon, David Densmore, William Dunlap, Jacob Yearmont.

(c) Spartanburg, Union.

110. JOHN LYNN 200

(b) Pl. Bk. 16, p. 362; 6 Jan. 1773; in Craven Co., bd'd John Ferguson, Charles Strong, Mary Gaston, vacant. cert. 11 Feb. 1773.

111. WILLIAM BARLOW 100

(b) P.F. 76; 6 Jan. 1773; to William Barlow 150 [6] acres, in Craven Co., south side of Broad River on waters of Cannan Creek; bd'd north and west by Abraham Thomson, east by John Barlow, south by Mariah Elizabeth Gross; sur. 29. Jan. 1773. (Dd 22 Oct. 1774 to Sec'ry. Recorded in Record of Plots, vol. 1, p. 135.)

(c) Newberry, Lexington.

112. SARAH REA 100

(b) P.F. 1572; 6 Jan. 1773; in Craven Co. south fork of Broad River on Gastons Branch of Turkey Creek; sur. 25 June 1773.

---

[6] The Council Journal clearly gives the name as "William," and the acreage to which he is entitled as 100 acres. However, the survey states there was laid off for him 150 acres bounded in part by John Barlow's land, and at the same time 100 acres were laid off for John Barlow on a precept for survey dated 6 January 1773. John Barlow is not listed as being given land at this time. He was already in South Carolina. He may already have had land and William had bought or been given 50 acres of it and it was divided at the time William's land was laid off to him.

(c) Chester, York.

113. FRANCES REA 200

(b) P.F. 1572; 6 Jan. 1773; in Craven Co. on Rocky Creek; bd'd
Thomas Blair, Alexander Walker, widow Steel, Alexander Hendry,
Thomas Houston; sur. 5 April 1773.

(c) Chester.

(d) Chester Co. Deed Bk. F, p. 216; Francis Rea on 29 Dec. 1797
sells above described 200 acres to William Paul of Chester Co.

York Will Bk. 1, p. 351; Francis Rea, 2 Feb. 1804, pr. 8 Aug.
1805, residing on Crowders Creek, York District; wife Sarah; sons:
William, Alexander, Francis; daughters: Mary, Elizabeth, Sarah;
granddaughter Rachel Jamison. Exs.: son John and John Henry.

114. GEORGE McMASTER 150

(b) P.F. 1227; 6 Jan. 1773; in Granville Co. on branch of Sawneys
Creek, waters of Savannah; bd'd land laid out for John Stephenson;
sur. 5 Feb. 1773.

(c) Abbeville.

115. PATRICK McMASTER 100

(b) P.F. 1228; 6 Jan. 1773; in Granville Co. on branch of Beargarden
Creek, waters of Savannah River; bd'd Hugh McMasters, Jean Cunningham; sur. 14 Feb. 1773.

(c) Abbeville.

116. JOHN McMASTER 100

(b) P.F. 1227; 5 Jan. 1773; in Colleton Co., spring branch of northwest fork of Long Cane; bd'd Frederick Ashmor, Jean Young, Moses
Thompson, John Smith; sur. 18 Feb. 1773.

(c) Abbeville.

117. HUGH McMASTER 100

(b) P.F. 1227; 6 Jan. 1773; in Granville Co. on waters of Bear
Garden Creek, a branch of Savannah River; bd'd land laid out for Wm.
McMaster and Jno. Stephenson; sur. 6 Feb. 1773.

(c) Abbeville.

(d) But see Fairfield Co. Wills, vol. 1, Bk. 1, p. 24. Will dated
19 July 1787, pr. 16 Nov. 1787 of Hugh McMaster, late of Parish of
Ballymoney, Co. Antrim, Kingdom of Ireland; passenger on Friendship
of Greenock in North Britain, last from Larne in Co. Antrim. On
leaving South Carolina May 1785 gave power of attorney to William
Dunlap and Arthur Morrow in 96 Dist., Long Cane settlement; to
brother John now in Ballymoney 100 acres if he comes over; child wife
now goes with, if it lives and comes of age; wife Margaret Killock;
brother-in-law James Killock (now on ship with me); sister Mary
McMaster. Refers to 100 acres and 50 acres in Long Cane settlement

to be sold, £20 of proceeds to Society of Reformed Presbyterians or Covenanters—settled in 96 Dist. Ex.: brother-in-law James Kinloch and Hugh McMullen. Refer to linen left with Mary Boyd in Long Cane to be sold.

118. MARTHA McMASTER 100

(b) P.F. 1228; 6 Jan. 1773; in Granville Co., on branch of Long Cain; bd'd John Patteson, Wm. Pattison; sur. 17 Feb. 1773.

(c) Abbeville.

119. NINIAN GREG 250

(b) Mem. vol. 2, p. 274; on branches of Turkey Creek; bd'd vacant land; survey cert. 30 Sept. 1774; granted to memorialist 17 March 1775.

(c) Chester, York.

120. ARCHIBALD McKEWN 250

(b) P.F. 1222; 5 Jan. 1773; to Archibald KcKown; in Colleton Co., on Colesons Branch, a branch of Little Saltcatchers Swamp; sur. 7 May 1773.

(c) Barnwell, Beaufort.

121. JOHN McKEWN 100

(b) P.F. 1216; 6 Jan. 1773; in Colleton Co. on head of Horsepen Bay; bd'd James Thompson; sur. 17 June 1774.

(c) Beaufort, Colleton.

122. MARY McKEWN 100

(b) P.F. 1216; 6 Jan. 1773; in Colleton Co. on Horsepen Bay; sur. 22 June 1773.

(c) Beaufort, Colleton.

123. GEORGE DARAGH 200

(b) P.F. 416; 6 Jan. 1773; in Colleton Co. on Calison's Branch, a branch of Little Saltcatchers Swamp; bd'd Archibald McKown and Moses Bennet; sur. 7 May 1773.

(c) Barnwell, Beaufort.

(d) But see Laurens Co. Wills, vol. 1, Bk. E-38.

124. ROBERT COWAN 350

(b) P.F. 372; 6 Jan. 1773; in Craven Co. on Rocky Creek; bd'd Mr. Morris, Ralph Baker; John McKoun, Thos. Stone, Robert McClurkan; cert. 19 May 1773.

(c) Chester.

125. JAMES CRAIG 100

(b) P.F. 377; 6 Jan. 1773; on northeast sides of Great Lynches Creek; bd'd vacant land, in Craven Co.; sur. 6 May 1773.

(c) Chesterfield, Lancaster, Kershaw.

126. MARY CRAIG 100

    (b) P.F. 378; 25 Jan. 1773; in Pinetree Dist. on waters of Sawneys Creek; bd'd Peter Crea; sur. 22 May 1773.

    (c) Fairfield, Kershaw.

127. JOHN CRAIG 100

    (b) P.F. 378; 6 Jan. 1773; in Craven Co. on branch of Linches Creek waters; sur. 27 Jan. 1773.

    (c) Kershaw

    (d) Kershaw Co. Wills, vol. 1, Bk. 1-A, p. 200; John Craig, 29 Aug. 1785. To Jennet Bonner, daughter to John Bonner; to "cuzen" William Craige "my loom," to "cuzen" John Bonner, who is residuary legatee and executor.

128. MARY GREG 100

    (b) P.F. 746; 6 Jan. 1773; in Craven Co., fork of Broad and Tyger Rivers on waters of Cane Creek; bd'd Isaac Cook, Thomas Shockley; sur. 25 Feb. 1773.

    (c) Union, Newberry.

129. RICHARD WRIGHT 150

    (b) P.F. 2071; 6 Jan. 1773; in Craven Co., south side Broad River on waters of Cannan Creek; bd'd Jacob Buzzard, Wm. Elmore, Jno. Robertson, Jane Kees, Sam'l McConnal; sur. 24 Feb. 1773.

    (c) Newberry, Lexington.

130. WILLIAM GREG 150

    (b) P.F. 747; 6 Jan. 1773; in Craven Co., south side Broad River, 95 acres on waters of Cannon Creek; bd'd Samuel McConnel, Matthias Kinard, Henry Hagel, Fogel Sang, John Stephenson; 30 Sept. 1774; 55 acres bd'd James Brown, Margaret Wilson.

    (c) Newberry, Lexington.

131. THOMAS WEIR 150

    (b) P.F. 1975; 6 Jan. 1773; to Thomas Weir, Sen'r.; in Craven Co., northwest side of Enoree River on branch called Beaver Dam; sur. 5 Feb. 1773.

    (c) Spartanburg, Union, possibly Laurens.

132. DAVID WEIR 100

    (b) P.F. 1975; 6 Jan. 1773; southwest side of Durbans Creek on small branch; bd'd James McClurkam, sen'r., Thomas Weir; sur. 8 Feb. 1773.

    (c) Laurens.

    (d) See Chester Co. deeds and also will, vol. 1, Bk. A, p. 135, 27 April 1797.

133. THOS. WEIR 100

(b) P.F. 1975; 6 Jan. 1773, to "Thos. Weir, Jr'r."; in Craven Co. northeast side of Rayburn's Creek on a small branch; bd'd William Williamson, Esq.; sur. 9 Feb. 1773.

(c) Laurens.

134. JOHN WEIR 100

(b) P.F. 1975; 6 Jan. 1773; in Craven Co. on waters of Reaburns Creek; bd'd by John Hellims; sur. 13 April 1773.

(c) Laurens Co. Deed Bk. B, p. 166; 28 Dec. 1786. Hastings Doyall and Rebecca his wife sold above land, which he had bought from John Weir 29 Oct. 1786.

(d) (See also Chester Co. Deeds and Wills.)

135. ARCHIBALD MCNEIL 250

136. JAMES SMITH 150

137. MARY STUART 100

138. JOHN GELASPY 100

(b) Pl. Bk., vol. 16, p. 74; 6 Jan. 1773; to John Galesby; in Craven Co.; bd'd Robert Montgomery; vacant land; sur. 25 Jan. 1773.

(c) Chester, Fairfield, York.

(d) Possibly Chester Co. Wills vol. 1, Bk. G, p. 25; John Galespie, 1 Dec. 1808, pr. March 1808; wife Sara, son James, daughter Mary Rodman; children of sons Thomas and James, and son-in-law Alexander Kell (gives details of grandchildren, etc.).

139. ALEXANDER MCMULLEN 100

(b) P.F. 1230; 5 Jan. 1773; in St. Marks Parish, Craven Co., in forks on Congaree and Wateree on west side of Cow Creek; sur. 20 June 1773.

(c) Richland.

140. JAMES TWEED 100

(b) P.F. 1905; 6 Jan. 1773; in Craven Co., northeast side Reyburn's Creek on small branch called Lick Creek; sur. 21 March 1773.

(c) Laurens.

141. ELEANOR TWEED 100

(b) P.F. 1905; 6 Jan. 1773; in Craven Co., 96 District, on branch of Reyburn's Creek called Bullet Branch; bd'd Thomas Hasker; sur. 5 March 1773.

(c) Laurens.

142. ROBERT TOAD [35] 100

(b) P.F. 1880; 6 Jan. 1773; in 96 District between Broad and Saluda Rivers, on small branch of Williamson Creek, waters of Reburn Creek from thence to Saluda; bd'd John Helams, Sr., Patrick Cunningham, Esq.; sur. 29 March 1773.

(c) Anderson, Laurens.

143. MARG'T TOAD 100

(b) Pl. Bk. vol. 20, p. 362; 6 Jan. 1773; in Craven Co., east side Reyburns Creek, on small branch called Reynolds Branch; bd'd John Richie; sur. 18 March 1773.

(c) Laurens.

144. ANDREW ERVING [36] 100

(b) P.F. 554; 6 Jan. 1773; in forks of Little River and Broad River in Craven Co.; bd'd Wm. Erving, John Thompson, Patrick Smith, vacant; sur. 9 Feb. 1773.

(c) Fairfield, Richland.

145. JOHN ERVING 100

(b) P.F. 555; 6 Jan. 1773; north side Broad River on branch of Little River in Camden Dist.; bd'd Richard Nealley, Thomas Woodard, Barnet Ellit, William Richardson, vacant land; sur. 13 Feb. 1773.

(c) Fairfield, Richland.

146. JANNET ERVING 100

(b) P.F. 554; 6 Jan. 1773, to Jannet Ewing; in forks of Little and Broad Rivers, Craven Co.; bd'd Edward McGraw, Jesse Foard, vacant land; sur. 9 Feb. 1773.

(c) Richland.

147. ELIZABETH ERVING 100

(b) P.F. 554; 6 Jan. 1773; 65 acres in fork of Saludy and Broad in Craven Co., bd'd John Thompson, Samuel McKee, Joseph Gibson; sur. 9 Feb. 1773. Also: 35 acres in fork of Little and Broad Rivers, Craven Co., bd'd Alex. Dealey, Jno. Hunt, Jno. Thompson.

(c) Newberry.

148. JEAN ERVING 100

(b) P.F. 554; 6 Jan. 1773; 100 acres in forks of Broad and Little Rivers in Craven Co.; bd'd Janet Erving, Edward McGraw, Andrew Erving, James Gibson; sur. 9 Feb. 1773.

(c) Fairfield, Richland.

149. ANDREW YOUNG 250

(b) P.F. 2081; 6 Jan. 1773; 100 acres, part of warrant on waters of Thickety Creek in Craven Co., bd'd Jasper Rogers, Mary Harport, John Addams; sur. 6 May 1774; also: 6 Jan. 1773; 150 acres remainder of warrant, in Craven Co. on branch of Little River; bd'd Irish land, Howel's land, vacant land; sur. 8 May 1773.

(c) Spartanburg, York, Fairfield.

150. JAMES VARNER 300

151. WM. YOUNG 100

(b) P.F. 2091; 5 Jan. 1773; on waters of Little River, on Hauts Branch, Craven Co.; sur. 7 Feb. 1773.

(c) Fairfield, Laurens, Newberry.

152. ISABEL YOUNG 100

(b) P.F. 2083; 6 Jan. 1773; in Craven Co., Hourts Branch; bd'd William Young; sur. 7 Feb. 1773.

(c) Fairfield, Laurens, Newberry.

153. JANET YOUNG 100

(b) P.F. 2084; 6 Jan. 1773; in Craven Co., on Little River; bd'd Joseph Lord; sur. 2 Feb. 1773.

(c) Fairfield, Laurens, Newberry.

154. MARY YOUNG 100

(b) P.F. 2087; 6 Jan. 1773; on Londonbridge Creek; 96 District; sur. 20 May 1773.

155. ROBERT KARNAHAN 250

(b) P.F. 1001; 6 Jan. 1773; in Craven Co., Camden Dist. on Bever Dams; bd'd James Pugsley, John Gaston; sur. 22 May 1773.

(c) Kershaw.

156. GILBERT REED 400

(b) P.F. 1576; 5 Jan. 1773; 289 acres in Berkeley Co., on waters of Indian Creek; bd'd William Waddle, Thomas Stark, Van Davis, William Willson, Harmon Davis, Tho. Stark; sur. 25 May 1773.

157. HUGH REED 100

(b) Pl. Bk.; vol. 20, p. 58; 5 Jan. 1773; in Craven Co., on two small branches of Indian Creek, waters of Enoree River; bd'd Sam'l Kelly, vacant land; sur. 2 March 1773.

(c) Laurens, Newberry.

158. MARGARET BEARD 100

(b) P.F. 95; 5 Jan. 1773; in Craven Co. on small branch of Indian Creek, waters of Enoree River; bd'd Joshua Reeder; land surveyed for John Beard, unknown and vacant land; sur. 3 March 1773.

(c) Laurens, Newberry.

159. EDMUND HOOLL 450

(b) P.F. 883; 6 Jan. 1773; between Gils and Hannah's Creeks; bd'd Capt. John Barkley survey; sur. 22 Jan. 1773.

(c) York.

160. CHARLES BRYNES 100

(b) P.F. 229; 6 Jan. 1773; on south branch of Camp Creek, on branch called "ye gread meadow"; bd'd vacant land; cert. 5 June 1773.

(c) Lancaster, York.

161. JOHN McNARY 100

(b) P.F. 1232; 6 Jan. 1773; Craven Co.; bd'd Gilbert McNary, Alex. McNary, And'w Rogers; sur. 11 Feb. 1773.

(c) Laurens.

162. ALEX'R McNARY 100

(b) P.F. 1232; 6 Jan. 1773; in Craven Co., on Dunkins Creek on branch called Beards Fork; bd'd John McNary.

(c) Laurens.

163. ANDREW WILSON 100

(b) P.F. 2027; 6 Jan. 1773; on north branch of Gils Creek, Waxhaw settlement; bd'd David Usher, William Robison; sur. 17 May 1773.

(c) York.

164. DAN'L WILSON 100

(b) P.F. 2027; 6 Jan. 1773; on Rising Springs water of Kane Creek, Waxhaw settlement; bd'd William Guthrie; sur. 29 Feb. 1773.

(c) Lancaster.

165. AGNES WILSON 100

(b) P.F. 2027; 6 Jan. 1773; north side Camp Creek, Waxhaw settlement; bd'd James Strain, John Strain, Jr., Arch'd McClemagh, Thos. Campbell, John Strain, Sr.; sur. 15 Jan. 1773.

(c) Lancaster.

166. WILLIAM TEAT 100

(b) P.F. 1848; 5 Jan. 1773; on both sides Little Lynches Creek in Parish of St. Marks, Craven Co.; bd'd Dan'l Williams, Mr. Wiley; sur. 6 April 1773.

(c) Lancaster, Kershaw.

167. JAMES SPEAR 100

(b) P.F. 1771; 6 Jan. 1773; in Colleton Co., on Mountain Creek branch of Turkey Creek; sur. 12 Feb. 1773.

168. LILLIAS CHAMBERS 100

(b) P.F. 312; 6 Jan. 1773; in Craven Co. on Bever Dam Branch; bd'd Mr. Barber's land, Jas. Valentine, Abner Ratree; sur. 23 April 1773.

(c) Kershaw.

169. ELIZABETH SHEILD 100

(b) P.F. 1702; 6 Jan. 1773; to Elizabeth Shield; in 96 District, waters of Cannon Creek, south side Broad River; bd'd Michael Rigard, Martin Lewiston, George Smith, Moses Kirkelin, Eliezer; sur. 26 Feb. 1773.

(c) Newberry, Lexington.

170. JOHN McCALASTER 100

(b) Pl. Bk. vol. 18; 6 Jan. 1773; in Burgley Co., Orangeburg Dist.

on Bucks Branch, waters of the four holes; bd'd ——— Myer, vacant land; sur. 10 April 1773.

(c) Berkeley, Orangeburg, Dorchester.

171. JOHN JOHNSTON 100

(b) P.F. 975; 5 Jan. 1773; in Craven Co., on headwaters of Linches Creek; sur. 28 June 1773.

(c) Lancaster, Chesterfield.

172. MARGARET CRAIG 100

(b) P.F. 378; 6 Jan. 1773; on north side of Camp Creek, waters of Cautawba River, Waxhaw settlement; bd'd by Jno. Craig, Sr., vacant land; sur. 1 Feb. 1773.

(c) Lancaster, York.

173. JOHN CORK 150

(b) Pl. Bk. 14, p. 195; 5 Jan. 1773; on north side Broad River, head of Brushy Fork of Little River, Craven Co.; bd'd Robert Ellison, sur. 23 March 1773.

(c) Fairfield.

(d) Fairfield Co. Will Bk., vol. 1, Bk. 2, p. 31. John Cork, 9 Feb. 1798, pr. 23 July 1798; wife Elizabeth, son-in-law and daughter Robert and Mary Casey; daughters: Margaret, Isabel and Elizabeth; sons: John and James, and son William (under age).

174. WILL'M McMASTER 100

(b) P.F. 1228; 6 Jan. 1773; in Granville Co., waters of Beargarden Creek, branch of Savannah River; sur. 5 Feb. 1773.

175. RACHEL ADAMS 100

176. AGNES HANNAH 100

177. MATHEW FLEMING 100

(b) Possibly Pl. Bk. vol. 15, p. 172; 25 May 1774; in Clarendon Co. on Pudden swamp; bd'd John Tonlin, Jacob Wooter, vacant land; cert. 11 Nov. 1774.

(c) Clarendon.

178. SARAH KIDD 100

(b) P.F. 1028; 6 Jan. 1773; in Craven Co., branch of Indian Creek, waters of Enoree River; bd'd Moses Kirkland, Henry Davis, James Steward; sur. 3 March 1773.

(c) Laurens and Newberry.

179. ELIZ'TH FLEMING 100

(b) P.F. 591; 25 May 1774; in forks of Black River, on Boggy Gulley; bd'd James Montgomery, Roger Wilson; sur. 18 July 1774.

(c) Sumter, Kershaw.

(d) See also Sumter Co. Wills, vol. 1, Bk. 2-D-1, p. 134; Elizabeth

Fleming, 26 May 1830, pr. 26 July 1830; Nephew Hamilton Bradley "now living in the Western Country"; niece Sarah G. Fleming; brother John Fleming.

180. JOHN McMURRAY 200

(b) P.F. 1231; 5 Jan. 1773; southwest side of Lynches Creek; bd'd Matth' Huggin, John Hays, George Underwood, Sr.; sur. 3 June 1773.

(c) Lancaster, Kershaw, Sumter, Williamsburg.

181. JOHN SEMPLE 250

(b) P.F. 1689; 6 Jan. 1773; in Craven Co. on Dry Fork of Dutchmans Creek; sur. 10 Feb. 1773.

(c) Fairfield, York, Spartanburg, Union.

182. ROWLIN MINLIN 100

183. JOHN McCALASTER 100

(b) Mem. v. 2, p. 296, 100 acres, Orangeburg Twp. on Buck Branch, waters of four holes, on Myers. Survey cert. 30 Sept. 1774; granted to Memorialist 17 March 1775.

(c) Orangeburg, Dorchester.

184. JAMES WILSON 200

(b) P.F. 2030; 6 Jan. 1773; on east side Linches, 3 miles above Ratcliff Bridge; bd'd Michael Mickson, John Mickson, Thomas Hardyman; sur. 27 Jan. 1773.

Ordered that the Secretary do prepare warrants of survey as prayed for the several petitioners.

* * *

A List of Passengers on Board the Hopewell arrived in South Carolina and this day petitioned for land, vizt.—

185. ALEXANDER McKEE 300

(b) P.F. 1209; 6 Jan. 1773; on south side Bever Creek, Craven Co.; bd'd Walter Shapshaw, Luke Petty; sur. 3 Feb. 1773.

(c) Lancaster.

186. JOSEPH GREEN 250

187. JOHN PATERSON 250

(b) No survey or memorial found but is possibly the John Patterson who died in 1776, then of 96 District. Examination of deeds and records of persons mentioned in the following referenced will may identify him.

(c) Charleston Wills, Bk. 18 (typed p. 238); John Patterson of 96 Dist., 25 August 1776; wife Sophia; children William and Sarah to be educated. Ex.: Brother George Patterson; wit. Edw'd Keating, Wm. Hutton.

188. ROBERT McCREE 250

(b) P.F. 1177; 3 Jan. 1773; in Craven Co., on Beaver Dam and branch of Crowders Creek; bd'd James Garden; sur. 25 Jan. 1773.

(c) Kershaw, York

189. SAMUEL DUNLAP 250

(b) P.F. 505; 6 Jan. 1773; in Craven Co., north of Rayburns Creek on branch; sur. 3 Feb. 1773.

(c) Laurens.

(d) Laurens Co. Wills, vol. 1, Bk. A, p. 43; Samuel Dunlap, 5 Feb. 1791; wife Nancy; sons: John, James; daughters: Catherine Dunlap, Suzanna Dunlap; 3 youngest daughters, Sarah, Nancy, Mary.

190. WILLIAM GIBSON 350

(b) P.F. 684; 6 Jan. 1773, in Craven Co., on southwest side of Scapeo'er Swamp on Home Branch; sur. 16 June 1774.

191. JAMES GIBSON 100

(b) P.F. 680; 3 Feb. 1773; in Camden Dist., branch of south fork of Turkey Creek; bd'd Alexander Harper, Jno. Kelley, William Barrows and his own line; sur. 9 Feb. 1773.

(c) York, Chester.

(d) (May be the James Gibson whose will is in York Co. Will Bk. 1; p. 322, 2 Dec. 1803, p. 9 March 1807; wife Martha; sons: James, William, Joseph, Thomas; daughters: Margaret, Jean, Martha. (Alexander Harper's will is also in York Co.)

192. JAMES GIBSON 150

193. NICHOLAS GIBBONS 250

(b) P.F. 676; 6 Jan. 1773; in Craven Co. on east side of Catawba River on waters of Camp Creek; bd'd by vacant land; sur. 18 July 1774.

(c) Lancaster.

194. JOHN KIRKPATRICK 350

(b) P.F. 1043; 6 Jan. 1773; 218 acres in Craven Co. on branch of Cane Creek; bd'd John McDows, James Barret, James Crams, Henry Hays, John Grieves, John James, James Mars; sur. 29 March 1773 (no more vacant land).

(c) Lancaster.

"N.B. Those above the line able to pay for their warrants."

195. JAMES MCKEE 100

(b) P.F. 1209; 6 Jan. 1773; on branch of Cedar Creek, east side Wateree River, Craven Co.; bd'd And'w McNutt; sur. 6 Mar. 1773.

(c) Lancaster.

196. CHARLES MCLELLAND 150

(b) P.F. 1162; 6 Jan. 1773; in Barkley Co., to Charles McClelland; between Broad and Shalluday Rivers, drains of Bare Creek; bd'd Peter Bayer; sur. 17 Jan. 1773.

(c) Newberry, Laurens, Union, Spartanburg.

197. JOHN PATERSON 100

(b) P.F. 1471; 6 Jan. 1773; in Craven Co., waters of Black Mingo; bd'd John Packer; sur. 25 May 1773.

(c) Williamsburg.

198. WILLIAM PATERSON 350

(b) Pl. Bk. vol. 19; 6 Jan. 1773; to William Beterson, in Craven Co., north side Lynches Creek; bd'd vacant land; cert. 15 May 1774.

(c) Chesterfield, Darlington, Florence.

199. AGNES PATERSON 350

(b) P.F. 1469; 6 Jan. 1773; 100 acres in Craven Co. on branch of Boggy Swamp, waters of Black Mingo; bd'd John Packer; sur. 28 May 1773.

(c) Williamsburg.

"The undernamed persons are not able to pay for their warrants." [7]

200. WILLIAM BRYSON 350

(b) P.F. 229; 6 Jan. 1773; on Red Bank Creek, waters of Little Saludy River in 96 Dist.; bd'd William McBride, Zachariah Davis; sur. 17 Feb. 1773.

(c) 96: Newberry, Laurens, Etc.

201. THOMAS GRAY 150

(b) P.F. 736; 6 Jan. 1773; in Granville Co. on Mounting Creek, waters of Turkey Creek; sur. 22 Feb. 1773.

(c) York, Chester.

202. ARCHIBALD GRAY 250

(b) P.F. 734; 6 Jan. 1773; in Granville Co. on Mounting Creek, the waters of Turkey Creek; bd'd Jacob Huffman, Jefferson Williams; sur. 22 Feb. 1773.

(c) York, Chester.

203. SAMUEL McCANCE 100

(b) P.F. 1159; 6 Jan. 1773; to "Samuel McCants"; in Craven Co., on the southwest side of Black Creek; bd'd George Smith; sur. 25 June 1773.

(c) Kershaw, Darlington.

(d) Probably writer of letter recorded in Sumter Co. Will Bk. 1-AA, p. 79; dated Turkey Creek, 1 May 1817 to "Dear Sister," designating her as his heir.

204. JOHN McCANCE 100

(b) Possibly P.F. 1159; 6 Jan. 1773; to "John McCants"; in Craven Co. east side of Sparrows Swamp; sur. 27 May 1773.

---

[7] This sentence is at the top of the Council Journal page and obviously refers to the "line" on the preceding page, so therefore includes the names below the line on the preceding page, that is, beginning with No. 195.

(c) Darlington. But see No. 10.

205. GEORGE WIN 100

206. ROBERT SMITH 350

207. SAMUEL CLARK 450

208. JAMES MCBRIDE 300

(b) P.F. 1154; 6 Jan. 1773; in Belfast township, 96 Dist.; bd'd William Dare, John Bell; sur. 10 March 1773.

(c) Abbeville.

209. ANN MCCREE 100

(b) P.F. 1176; 6 Jan. 1773; on Bulocks Creek, Camden Dist.; bd'd Wm. Dunlap, James Watson, Wm. Burns; sur. 16 April 1773.

(c) York.

210. SARAH MCCREE 100

(b) Pl. Bk. 18, p. 173; 6 Jan. 1773; to Sarah McRee; in Camden Dist., north side Allison's Creek; bd'd Ezekiel Polk, William Davidson, John Kerr, vacant land; sur. 26 April 1773.

(c) York.

211. SUSANNAH MCCREE 100

(b) P.F. 1177; 6 Jan. 1773; in Camden Dist., north side Allison's Creek; bd'd Thomas Olerk; sur. 27 April 1773.

(c) York.

212. ALEXANDER MCCREE 100

(b) P.F. 1177; 6 Jan. 1773; in Camden Dist., north side Absons Creek; bd'd Thomas Banks; sur. 26 April 1773.

(c) York.

213. JAMES GRACY 250

(b) P.F. 726; 6 Jan. 1773; on branches of Flat Creek in Parish of St. Marks in Craven Co., bd'd Joshua Hickman; sur. 31 March 1773.

(c) Lancaster.

214. JOHN GRACY 100

(b) Pl. Bk. vol. 16, p. 172; 6 Jan. 1773; on branch of Beaver Creek, in Craven Co.; bd'd John Brown, Mary Gracy, vacant land; cert. 25 March 1773.

(c) Fairfield, Lancaster.

215. ROBERT GRACY 100

216. MARY GRACY 100

(b) P.F. 727; 6 Jan. 1773; on Cedar Creek, in Craven Co.; bd'd John Brown, John Gracy; sur. 8 April 1773.

(c) Fairfield, Lancaster.

217. MARTHA GIBENEY 100

(b) Pl. Bk. vol. 16, p. 58, 6 Jan. 1773; to Martha Gibeny, on Clarks

Fork of Bullocks Creek; bd'd William McElwes (on plat as "McClewes");
sur. 3 May 1773.

(c) York.

218. WILLIAM MILLER 200

219. ROBERT HAMILTON 250

(b) P.F. 783; 6 Jan. 1773; in Craven Co. on Black River; bd'd James
Armstrong, Moses Gordon; sur. 8 June 1774.

(c) Darlington, Sumter, Williamsburg.

220. HUGH THOMSON 350

(b) Pl. Bk. vol. 20, p. 322; 6 Jan. 1773; to Hugh Thompson; on
branches of Grannys Quarter in Craven Co.; bd'd Mrs. McQuatty, W.
McKee, vacant land; sur. 25 May 1773.

(c) Kershaw.

(d) Possibly testator recorded in Charleston Wills, Bk. 16, p. 372;
Hugh Thomson of Craven Co. 5 May 1775; son William, daughter Sarah
Ann Thomson (500 acres purchased of John Cross), both under age of
20; brother James Thomson. Ex.: brother, friends Peter Kolb, Thomas
Pitts, John Potts.

221. WILLIAM DUNLAP 200

(b) P.F. 505; 6 Jan. 1773; branch of Grannys Quarter, Craven Co.;
bd'd Mr. Fleming, Mr. Watson, Michael Ganters (?); sur. 15 Jan. 1774.

(c) Kershaw.

222. ROBERT DUNLAP 150

(b) P.F. 504; 6 Jan. 1773; on branches of Grannys Quarter Creek in
Parish of St. Marks, Craven Co.; bd'd James McGally; sur. 10 March
1773.

(c) Kershaw.

223. DANIEL MCMULLEN 100

(b) P.F. 1230; 6 Jan. 1773; 85 acres on branch of Grannys Quarter
Creek, north side of Wateree River in Craven Co.; bd'd Stephen
Matlocks, Sam'l Milhaus, Arch'd Watson; sur. 2 March 1773.

(c) Kershaw.

224. JAMES YOUNG 100

(b) Precept for two surveys of 100 acres each were made the same
day for "James Young," obviously two different men. Which of these
was for the passenger in the Hopewell has not been determined. Further
examination of county and other records may clarify this. Following
are the two surveys:

P.F. 2084; 6 Jan. 1773; 100 acres in Craven Co., south side of Enoree
on waters of Indian Creek; all sides vacant land; sur. 6 Feb. 1773.

P.F. 2084; 6 Jan. 1773; 100 acres in Barkley Co., between Broad and

Shalluday, on small dreen of Wateree Creek; sur. 17 Jan. 1773; bd'd Adam Summers, vacant.

225. JOHN CLARKE 100

(b) P.F. 333; 6 Jan. 1773; to John Clark; on south side of 12-mile creek, in Craven Co., bd'd John Drennen, Andrew Nuts, Jean Young; sur. 4 Feb. 1774.

(c) Lancaster (?).

226. WILLIAM BOYD 250

(b) P.F. 170; 6 Jan. 1773; 222 acres in Craven Co., on northeast side of Rayburns Creek; bd'd Samuel Williams, Phillip Sherrill; sur. 3 Feb. 1773.

(c) Laurens.

227. JOSEPH MENELLY 250

228. ROBERT GIBSON 100

(b) P.F. 684; 6 Jan. 1773; in Craven Co. on Pointy Stump Branch, waters of Indian Town Swamp and Black Mingo; sur. 28 May 1773.

(c) Williamsburg, Georgetown.

229. MARGARET GIBSON 100

(b) P.F. 682; 6 Jan. 1773; in Craven Co., West Branch of Poplar Hill Swamp, waters of Black Mingo; sur. 25 May 1773.

230. JOHN SHAW 100

(b) P.F. 1697; 6 Jan. 1773; in Craven Co., on Hopes Swamp; bd'd Will'm Cassel; sur. 20 June 1774.

(c) Sumter.

231. GEORGE GIBSON 400

232. JOHN SMITH 450

(b) P.F. 1751; 6 Jan. 1773; in Craven Co., on southwest side of Black Creek; bd'd George Smith; sur. 25 June 1773.

(c) Darlington.

233. GEORGE SMITH 100

(b) P.F. 1744; 6 Jan. 1773; in Craven Co., southwest side of Black Creek; bd'd Samuel McCants, John Smith; sur. 25 June 1773.

(c) Darlington.

234. ALEX'R DOUGLAS 800

(b) P.F. 498; 6 Jan. 1773; to Alexander Duglass; in Craven Co., south side of Black Creek; bd'd Lewis Davis, John Beard; sur. 19 May 1773, "Order of Council for Samuel, William, Margaret and Elizabeth Douglass, 17 June 1774."

(c) Darlington.

235. GEORGE THOMSON 100
     (b) P.F. 1866; 6 Jan. 1773; in Berkeley Co., of St. Matthews Parish
on Kittle Branch; sur. 23 June 1773.
     (c) Orangeburg.

236. JOHN BEARD 250
     (b) P.F. 96; 6 Jan. 1773; in Craven Co. on south side of Black
Creek; bd'd Alexander Duglis, vacant land; sur. 19 June 1773.
     (c) Darlington.

237. MARY SHEPHERD 100
     (b) P.F. 1700; 6 Jan. 1773; in Craven Co., on head of Black River;
bd'd John Fleming; sur. 7 May 1773.
     (c) Darlington.

238. WILLIAM SHANKS 400
     (b) P.F. 1694; 6 Jan. 1773; in Craven Co., on northwest side of Pee
Dee River near Catfish; sur. 5 June 1773.
     (c) Georgetown.

239. JOSEPH GRACEY 250
     (b) Pl. Bk. vol. 16, p. 175; 6 Jan. 1773; in Craven Co., on north
side of Lynches Lake on the Big Branch; bd'd Peter Pedden, James
Scott, vacant land; sur. 22 Jan. 1773.
     (c) Kershaw, Darlington, Florence.

240. ROBERT MATHEWS 300
     (b) P.F. 1270; 6 Jan. 1773; in Craven Co. on west side Lynches
Creek on 4-Mile Branch; sur. 13 Feb. 1773.
     (c) Kershaw, Darlington, Florence.

241. ELIZABETH MATHEWS 100
     (b) Pl. Bk. vol. 18, p. 51; 6 Jan. 1773; on north side Lynches Creek
and Muddy Creek, in Craven Co.; bd'd Robert McNight (plat reads
"McKnight"), Philip Owen, vacant land; cert. 6 March 1773.
     (c) Chesterfield, Darlington.

242. MARGARET MATHEWS 100
     (b) P.F. 1269; 6 Jan. 1773; in Craven Co. on waters of Muddy
Creek.
     (c) Chesterfield, Darlington.

243. JANET PATERSON 100
     (b) P.F. 1470; 6 Jan. 1773; to Jennet Patterson; in Craven Co., on
east side of Catawba River on waters of Cane Creek; bd'd David Leard;
sur. 8 June 1778.
     (c) Lancaster.

244. JAMES McCAULEY 100

245. ROBERT ALEXANDER 150

246. ALEX'R CRAIG 100

247. JOHN STEVENSON 150

(b) P.F. 1795; 6 Jan. 1773; in Berkeley Co. in fork between Broad River and Saludy, southwest side of Enoree; bd'd river, Thomas Gordon, John Odele; sur. 28 May 1773.

(c) Laurens.

(d) Laurens Deed Bk. F, p. 342, 20 Jan. 1791; sells above to John Robertson.

Ordered that the Secretary do prepare Warrants of Survey as prayed for by the several petitioners.

* * *

A List of Passengers arrived from Ireland in the ship **Pennsylvania Farmer** and this Day petitioned for Land vizt.—

248. JOHN LOGUE 400

(b) P.F. 1128; 6 Jan. 1773; in Craven Co., on branch of Congaree River, called Seader Creek; bd'd Elias Dake, Robert Evins, Martin Stroder, Jacob Dickson, Andrew Patterson; sur. 20 June 1773.

(c) Richland.

249. JAMES MOORE 300

(b) Pl. Bk. vol. 18, p. 501; 5 Jan. 1773; in Granville Co., near Savannah River; bd'd James Wilson, vacant land; cert. 4 July 1774.

(c) Abbeville.

250. JAMES PHILLIPS 250

(b) P.F. 1504; 6 Jan. 1773; north side Packlet River, branch of Thickety Creek; bd'd Ann Chesney, William Simes; sur. 3 June 1773.

(c) Spartanburg.

251. JOHN SMITH, Sen'r 250

(b) P.F. 1750; 6 Jan. 1773; in Craven Co. on branch of Rocky Creek; bd'd Elisha Garret, Matthew Grimbs, William Hood, Thomas Hickling, Jasper Roger; sur. 9 Feb. 1773.

(c) Chester, York.

252. ANDREW PATERSON 250

(b) P.F. 1468; 6 Jan. 1773; in Craven Co., drains of Seader Creek and waters of Congaree or Santee River; bd'd Elias Drake, John Pitman, Gonrad Hersh (or Kersh), Jacob Disicker; sur. 22 April 1773.

(c) Richland.

(d) Richland Wills, vol. 1, Bk. D, p. 1; Andrew Paterson, 24 August 1799, pr. 7 May 1800; sons: Samuel, James; dau. Elizabeth.

253. DAVID McCREIGHT 150

(b) P.F. 1177; 6 Jan. 1773; in Craven Co., on north side of Broad River on branch of Jacksons Creek; bd'd John Winn, Wm. McCreight, Wm. Owens; sur. 29 Jan. 1773.

(d) Fairfield Wills, vol. 1, Bk. 2, p. 70A. David McCreight, 5 Sept. 1779, pr. 18 July 1794; wife Mary; sons: James, John, Matthew, David; grandchildren: David, son of Davy; William, Robert, John, sons of William; Agnes and Mary, daughters of William, etc.

254. WILLIAM McCREIGHT 400

(b) P.F. 1175; 6 Jan. 1773; on branch of Jacksons Creek in Craven Co.; bd'd Wm. Trap, Wm. Ounes, David McCraight, John McCaw, Wm. Willson, James Porter, Thos. Phillips, John Phillips, John Harvey, Benjamin Ounes; sur. 20 Jan. 1773.

(c) Fairfield.

(d) Fairfield Wills, vol. 1, bk. 1, p. 26: William McCreight of Jacksons Creek, Parish of St. Marks, Craven Co.; 10 Nov. 1776, pr. 20 Jan. 1792; sons: Robert, David, William; daughters: Agnes, Mary; wife Agnes.

255. DAVID McCREIGHT 200

(b) P.F. 1177; 6 Jan. 1773; 100 acres (part of 200) in Craven Co., on branch of Wateree Creek on Charleston Road; bd'd Andrew Medows, Simon Kelly; sur. 6 June 1773.

Also 100 acres (balance of 200) in Craven Co., on north side of Broad River, on Susy Banks Branch of Turkey Creek; bd'd Turner Kendrick; sur. 6 June 1773.

(c) 1st Fairfield; 2nd Chester.

256. WILLIAM YOUNG 300

(b) P.F. 2091; 6 Jan. 1773; on Gills Creek, Craven Co.; bd'd John Belk, Sr., John Belk, Jr., John Barker; sur. 22 Jan. 1773.

(c) Richland, Lancaster.

257. WILLIAM WILLEY 350

(b) P.F. 2003; 6 Jan. 1773; in Craven Co. on head of Rocky Creek; bd'd William Willey, John Burns, John Gill, Mickel Dickson; sur. 15 March 1773.

(c) Chester.

(d) Chester Co. Wills, vol. 1, Bk. D, p. 15; William Willey, 4 Dec. 1799; pr. 11 Oct. 1806. Wife Margaret; sons: James, Joseph, William, Thomas, Samuel; daughters: Elizabeth Kenmore, Margret and Mary Wylie.

258. THOMAS SPENCE 350

(b) P.F. 1774; 6 Jan. 1773; on waters of Coffee Town Creek, in 96 Dist.; bd'd Wm. Campbell, Samuel Holladay, Nathaniel Henderson, John Hamilton, Isabel Walker, Francis Walker, William Walker, Thomas Walker, John McIntosh; sur. 19 March 1773.

(c) Edgefield.

259. ARCHIBALD TODD 250

(b) P.F. 1882; 6 Jan. 1773; in Colleton Co., 96 Dist., waters of 96 Creek; bd'd Jane Brownlee; sur. 7 Feb. 1773.

(c) Edgefield.

260. DAVID GRIMBS 400

261. NATHANIEL MCDILL 300

(b) P.F. 1185; 6 Jan. 1773; on Cedar Creek of Broad River in Craven Co.; bd'd Philip Showers, Richard Grodlicks, ———— Shots; sur. 15 Feb. 1773.

(c) Probably Richland or Fairfield.

(d) May be the testator recorded in typed copies of Kershaw Co. Wills vol. 1, wills not recorded, p. 67; Nathaniel McDill, 24 Sept. 1783, pr. 16 April 1785; wife "Meary"; "my seven children"; Overseers Thomas McDill and James Pedin.

262. JOHN COCHRAN 100

(b) Pl. Bk. vol. 14, p. 132; 6 Jan. 1773; in Craven Co.; bd'd James Rogers, Samuel Houston, vacant; sur. 25 Jan. 1773.

(c) Rogers land was on Rocky Creek, so Cochran land was in Chester or York.

263. SAMUEL MCCEE 100

(b) P.F. 1209; 6 Jan. 1773; to Samuel McKee, 100 acres in Craven Co. on north side Broad River, bd'd Joseph Gibson; sur. 9 Jan. 1779.

Royal Grants, Bk. 30, p. 249, to Samuel McKee, 100 acres in Craven Co. on north side Broad River on small branch 4 ft. wide and 4 inches deep; bd'd Joseph Gibson, vacant land; cert. 7 May 1774.

264. JOHN SMITH, Jun'r 100

(b) P.F. 1751; 6 Jan. 1773; in Craven Co. on branch of Mill Creek and waters of Little River; bd'd "suposed to belong to Mr. Posshees"; sur. 26 Feb. 1773.

(c) Fairfield.

(d) Possibly testator, Fairfield Will Bk. 2-14, p. 117.

265. JAMES FAIREY 100

(b) P.F. 559; 6 Jan. 1773; in Craven Co. on south fork of Little River of Broad River; bd'd John Walker.

(c) Fairfield, York.

266. DAVID DUNN 100

267. WILLIAM MCKEEN 100

(b) P.F. 1210; 6 Jan. 1773; in Granville Co. — Savannah River, Long Cane Settlement on Russell lower branch in 96 Dist.; bd'd William Caskey; sur. 19 Feb. 1773.

(c) Abbeville.

268. JAMES McCREIGHT 100

(b) Pl. Bk. vol. 18, p. 179; 6 Jan. 1773; on north side Broad, on south fork of Little River in Camden Dist.; bd'd Jno. Kelley, Jane Wagmore, Sam'l Maberly.

(c) Fairfield.

269. ANN YOUNG 100

(b) P.F. 2087; 6 Jan. 1773; on both sides Barkley Creek; bd'd Capt. John Barkley, John Belk; sur. "1st day ——— 1773."

(c) Lancaster.

270. FRANCIS ARTHBURTHENET 450

(b) Post Rev. Plats, Bundle 5, No. 130; 6 Jan. 1773; 450 acres to Francis Arbuthnet in Craven Co., Williamsburg Township; bd'd Roger McGill, Isaac Barrenow, Robert Lowrys, vacant land; cert. 24 March 1773. D'd. to Danil Mazyck 18 July 1774. Granted to Daniel Mazyck 17 July 1784.

The above are able to pay

The undermentioned are not able to pay

271. HUGH WAXON 350

272. SAMUEL GAMBLE 300

(b) Pl. Bk. vol. 16, p. 18; 6 Jan. 1773; in Camden Dist. on branch of Turkey Creek and waters of Broad River; bd'd Thomas Willson, vacant land; sur. 26 Aug. 1773.

(c) Chester, Fairfield.

273. JAMES HARBERSON 150

274. WILLIAM BROWN 400

(b) P.F. 219; 6 Jan. 1773; in Craven Co. on branch of Sandy River; bd'd Stephen Maxzek, Benjamin Carter, vacant land; sur. 19 Aug. 1773.

(c) Chester.

275. MOLLY McRORY 150

276. ROBERT CALLWELL 450

(b) Pl. Bk. vol. 13, p. 485; 6 Jan. 1773; to Robert Caldwell; in Berkly Co. on Beaver Dam Creek, branch of Saludy River; bd'd vacant land; sur. 14 Feb. 1773.

(c) Laurens, Abbeville, Pendleton, Newberry.

(d) See. No. 324.

277. THOMAS SCOTT 300

(b) P.F. 1679; 6 Jan. 1773; 260 acres in Craven Co. on waters of Wateree; bd'd Jacob Gray, James M. Gill, Thomas Carter; sur. 5 April 1773.

(c) Richland.

278. Samuel Hall 150

(b) P.F. 777; 2 Feb. 1773; 100 acres in Craven Co., on Peages Creek, waters of Little River; bd'd George Nelly, William Caldwell, Solomon Winter, Samuel Trartor, Robert Cunningham; sur. 21 June 1773.

Also: 2 Feb. 1773; 50 acres in Craven Co., waters of Little River; bd'd William Hambleton, James Phillpot; sur. 21 June 1773.

(c) Richland, Fairfield; or Newberry, Laurens.

279. Andrew Spence 300

(b) P.F. 1772; 6 Jan. 1773; in Barkley Co. on beach creek, waters of Saludy River; bd'd Jno. Boyd, Wm. Kelley, John Kelley; sur. 13 Feb. 1773.

280. Robert Spear 350

(b) P.F. 1771; 6 Jan. 1773; in Craven Co.; waters of Little River, on small branch called Beaver Dam branch; bd'd William Taylor, David Spence, Richard Robertson, Agnes Spence; sur. 12 Feb. 1773.

(c) Fairfield, Laurens, Newberry.

281. Henry Heerton 200

(b) Pl. Bk. vol. 15, p. 381; 6 Jan. 1773; to Henry Hearton; 104 acres in Craven Co., in fork between Broad and Little Rivers, on banks of Neely's Creek; bd'd Jno. Boyd, "estate of the Austins," Jacob Gibson, land surveys for Victor and Richard Neeley, John Long; sur. 22 Feb. 1773.

Also p. 381; 6 Jan. 1773, to same, 96 acres in Craven Co., on small branch of Rocky Creek, waters of Broad River; bd'd John Rowbuck, Jacob Canemore, Peter Rees, Thomas Davis, vacant land; sur. 25 March 1773.

(c) Fairfield, Chester.

282. James McMaster 250

(b) P.F. 1227; 6 Jan. 1773; 145 acres (part of warrant for 250) in Craven Co.; bd'd George Fouser, ——— Elieger, Matthias Koiner, Frederick Shener, Michael Kibler; sur. 30 June 1773.

Also: P.F. 1227; 6 Jan. 1773; 105 acres (remaining part) in 96 Dist. on waters of Camping Creek, north side of Saluda River, Craven Co.; sur. 2 July 1773.

(c) Newberry.

(d) Possibly testator whose will is in Newberry Wills, vol. 2, Bk. G, p. 19; James McMaster, 5 June 1819, pr. 12 July 1819. Dau. Mary Canard, son Thomas; heirs of daughters Ann McCrary, Janet Caldwell, and Rosannah Starks. Ex.: "son" John Starks.

283. James McConoughy 100

(b) P.F. 1171; 6 Jan. 1773; in 96 Dist. on branch of waters of Saludy River; bd'd Joseph Culbreath; sur. 1 July 1773.

(c) Newberry, Abbeville, Laurens, Anderson.

284. JOHN SPROLL 100

(b) P.F. 1779; 6 Jan. 1773; in fork between Congaree and Wateree on small prong of Dry Branch, being waters of Cedar Creek; bd'd Jonathan Wilkins; sur. 12 July 1774.

(c) Richland.

285. DAVID MILLER 300

(b) P.F. 1301; 6 Jan. 1773; on upper branches of Bever Creek, Parish of St. Marks, Craven Co., bd'd James Williams; sur. 25 March 1773.

286. JAMES MANN 200

(b) P.F. 1247; 6 Jan. 1773; in Craven Co., on Crooked Run; bd'd Stephen Elizer, David McGraw, Nicholas Miriek; sur. 6 Feb. 1773.

(c) Fairfield.

287. JAMES BARBER 250

(b) P.F. 73; 6 Jan. 1773; on Nixon Creek, Craven Co.; bd'd vacant land; sur. 24 Feb. 1773.

(c) Fairfield.

(d) Possibly brother of 319 John Barber, and is the testator whose will is in Fairfield Co. Wills, vol. 2, Bk. 9, p. 1; James Barber, 23 June 1824, pr. 27 April 1825; wife Sarah; son, Robert Gunning Barber; daughters Eliza Richmond, and Jane and her husband Hugh Barkley; grandsons James Barber Richmond and James Barber Barkley; nephew James Barber, son of John; James Barber Smith, son of William; James Barber McCully; brother John Barber.

288. MATHEW MEBIN 150

(b) Memorials, vol. 2, p. 288; 100 acres on Broad River on branch of Cannons Creek; bd'd John Buzzard, John McClelland, vacant land; cert. 30 Sept. 1774. Granted 17 March 1775 to Memorialist.

289. WILLIAM MEBIN 200

(b) Royal Grants, vol. 35, p. 434; in Craven Co. on branch of Fair Forest; bd'd Mary Leach; granted 17 March 1775.

(c) Union, Spartanburg.

290. JOHN McCRORY 100

(b) P.F. 1178; 6 Jan. 1773; between Camp Creek and Gils Creek, branch of Wateree River; Waxhaw Settlement; bd'd by Richard and John Cowsers, Thos. McCrory, John Galaspie; sur. 25 Jan. 1773.

(c) Lancaster.

291. ALEXANDER GASTON 100

(b) P.F. 654; 6 Jan. 1773; in Craven Co., waters of Fishing Creek, near the Indian line; sur. 16 April 1773.

(c) York.

292. JOHN STINSON 100

(b) P.F. 1795; 6 Jan. 1773, to "John Stevenson," in Craven Co.,
bd'd Wm. Hood; sur. 15 Jan. 1773.

(c) Fairfield.

(d) Fairfield Wills, vol. 1, 1781 and 1819; Bk. 5, p. 449. (Apt. 31;
File 481), dated 5 March 1808, proved 5 April 1808. John Stevenson of
Fairfield Dist.; wife, Jennet Stevenson; sons: William, James, Hugh,
John, Andrew, Robert, Samuel; Dau.: Margaret Stevenson. Exs.: Wife,
John Simonson, John Waugh. (Considerable information is available
about this man and some of his descendants.)

293. AGNES WALKER 100

(b) P.F. 1933; 6 Jan. 1773; on south side of Kane Creek (Long
Cane Settlement); bd'd Joseph Walker, John Montgomery; sur. 28 Jan.
1773.

(c) Lancaster.

294. JOHN MCMURRAY 100

(b) P.F. 1231; 6 Jan. 1773; branch on waters of Tiger River; bd'd
Robert Ouens, Michael Pratt; sur. 5 Feb. 1773.

(c) Spartanburg, Union.

295. JAMES HILL 100
296. ALEXANDER MCCAULEY 100
297. ELIZABETH STEEN 100

(b) Pl. Bk. vol. 21, p. 97; 6 Jan. 1773; in Craven Co., branch of
Rocky Creek; bd'd vacant land; sur. 28 Jan. 1773.

(c) Chester.

298. MARY LEECH 100

(b) P.F. 1081; 6 Jan. 1773; in Craven Co. on branches of Fair Forest;
bd'd William Mabin.

(c) Spartanburg, Union.

299. SAMUEL LOGUE 100

(b) P.F. 1128; 6 Jan. 1773; in Craven Co., on branch of Congaree
River called Seader Creek; bd'd J—— Willson; sur. 20 June 1773.

(c) Richland.

300. AGNES WAXEN 100

(b) P.F. 1966; 6 Jan. 1773; waters of Little River; bd'd James
Farye, Sam'l Maberly; sur. 14 July 1773.

(c) Fairfield, Laurens, Newberry.

301. ELIZABETH WAXON 100

(b) P.F. 1966; 6 Jan. 1773; waters of Little River; bd'd John Walker,
John Wagner; sur. 14 July 1773.

(c) Fairfield, Laurens, Newberry.

302. AGNES HERBESON 100

(b) Pl. Bk. 15, p. 287; 6 Jan. 1773; to Agness Harbison; in Craven Co. on small branch of Rocky Creek; bd'd Gasper Sliker, Kelly McKane, David Fairey, John Pike, vacant land; sur. 3 Feb. 1773.

(c) Chester.

303. MARY GASTON 100

(b) P.F. 665; 6 Jan. 1773; on Fishing Creek in Craven Co.; bd'd Hugh Gaston; sur. 7 July 1774.

(c) York, Chester.

304. JEAN YOUNG 100

(b) P.F. 2085; 6 Jan. 1773; in Craven Co., on 12-Mile Creek, 1 m. from Wagon ford; bd'd "ye waggon road which makes ye Province line," Thos. Drennen, John Taylor; sur. 20 June 1774.

(c) Lancaster.

305. MARRIAN McCOLLOUGH 100

(b) P.F. 1180; 6 Jan. 1773; to Mary Ann McCullough; in Craven Co., on branch of Cain Creek; bd'd Robert Ramsay, Donald Drennan; sur. 8 Feb. 1773.

(c) Lancaster.

306. MARY STINSON 100

(b) P.F. 1800; 6 Jan. 1773; Moors Branch, east side Kane Creek, Waxhaw Settlement; bd'd James Walker; sur. 28 Jan. 1773.

(c) Lancaster.

307. WILLIAM SCOTT 100

308. JOHN MILLER 100

(b) P.F. 1304; 6 Jan. 1773; in Craven Co., branch of Little Lynches Creek; sur. 27 Jan. 1773.

(c) Lancaster, Chesterfield, Kershaw.

309. ELIZ'TH MILLER 100

310. JAMES SPENCE 100

(b) P.F. 1773; 6 Jan. 1773; in Barkley Co., on Little Norton Creek, branch of Saludy River; bd'd bounty land, ——— Osewatt; sur. 11 March 1773.

(c) Abbeville.

311. MARY SPENCE 100

(b) P.F. 1774; 6 Jan. 1773; in Barkley Co. on Little Noton Creek, branch of Saludy; bd'd bounty land; sur. 15 Feb. 1773.

(c) Abbeville.

312. JEAN SPENCE 100

(b) P.F. 1773; 6 Jan. 1773; 70 acres being part of warrant for 100; in Barkley Co. on Dudleys Creek, Saludy River; bd'd Robert Cardwell,

John Jinkins. David Spence, John James, Adam McClanahan, Joseph Spence; sur. 12 Feb. 1773.

(c) Newberry.

313. JEAN TODD 100

(b) P.F. 1882; 6 Jan. 1773; in 96 Dist., waters of Sleepy Creek; bd'd Moses Kirkland, Thomas Youngblood; sur. 11 Feb. 1773.

314. MARTHA MEABIN 100

315. MARY MEABIN 100

(b) P.F. 1237; 6 Jan. 1773; in Craven Co. on branches of Fair Forest; bd'd vacant land; sur. 25 March 1773.

(c) Spartanburg.

316. JOHN BLEAR 100

(b) P.F. 141; 6 Jan. 1773, in Craven Co., Camden Dist., on great road leading from McDonald's Pond to Camden; bd'd vacant land; sur. 20 March 1773.

(c) Kershaw, Lancaster.

317. JOHN BROWN 100

(b) P.F. 211; 6 Jan. 1773; in Craven Co., on Rocky Creek; bd'd Robert Bailey, Hugh Parks, William Hickling; sur. 16 March 1773.

(c) Chester.

318. WILLIAM BROWN 100

(b) P.F. 219; 6 Jan. 1773; in Craven Co., on branch of Rocky Creek; bd'd Alexander Brady, Margaret Patten, vacant land; sur. 15 March 1773.

(c) Chester, Fairfield.

(d) Chester Co. Deed Bk. R, p. 350, 2 Feb. 1816, William Brown, Sr., of Fairfield District, Rocky Creek, sells to George Brown of Chester, 100 acres grant to William Brown, 9 Nov. 1774 (described as above). Wit.: John Brown, Elijah McCrary. Mary, wife of William, relinquishes her dower 19 Feb. 1816.

Chester Deed Bk. S, p. 56; 6 July 1816. William Brown and wife Molly Brown of Fairfield Co. appoint John McDonald of Chester Dist. to receive one part of estate of Hugh McDonald, dec'd of Chester Dist. Wit.: William Brown, Jr.

319. JOHN BARBER 100

(b) P.F. 73; 6 Jan. 1773; on Nickson's Branch, Craven Co., bd'd vacant land; sur. 3 April 1773.

(c) Fairfield.

320. ANDREW GRUMBS 100

(b) P.F. 756; 6 Jan. 1773; to Andrew Grimbs; in Craven Co. on branch of Rocky Creek; bd'd by James Knox, Francis Henderson, Benjamin Mitchell, —— Bione; sur. 1 July 1773.

(c) Chester.

321. JEAN GRIMBS 100

(b) P.F. 755; 6 Jan. 1773; in Craven Co., on branch of Rocky Creek; bd'd Samuel Fulton; sur. 1 Feb. 1773.

(c) Chester.

322. MATHEW GRIMBS ....,.............. 100

(b) P.F. 756; 6 Jan. 1773; in Camden Dist., waters of Rocky Creek; bd'd Alexander Turner, Samuel Wilson, John McDonald; sur. 7 May 1773.

(c) Chester.

323. WILLIAM CALDWELL 100

(b) Pl. Bk. vol. 13, p. 485; 6 Jan. 1773; in Berkley Co. on branch of Rocky Creek, waters of Saludy; bd'd Robert Caldwell, vacant land; cert. 15 Feb. 1773.

(c) Abbeville, Edgefield.

324. ROBERT CALDWELL 100

(b) Pl. Bk. vol. 13, p. 484; 6 Jan. 1773; in Berkeley Co. on Dudley Creek, a branch of Saludy River; bd'd John Jinken, Joseph Spence, vacant land; sur. 12 Feb. 1773.

(c) Newberry.

(d) This Robert Caldwell or No. 276 may be testator whose will is recorded in Newberry Wills, vol. 2, Book I, p. 7: Robert Caldwell, Sr., 28 Feb. 1781, pr. 9 Jan. 1823: Wife Gennet; sons: James, Robert, William, Dickson, Joseph, John; daughters: Mary Read, Gennet Chambers, Abigail Spence; wit.: James Sloan, George Caldwell.

325. ANNE CALDWELL 100

(b) P.F. 261; 6 Jan. 1773; on branch of Wateree Creek; bd'd John Thompson, Hugh Smith; sur. 10 June 1773.

(c) Fairfield.

326. AGNES ELLIOTT 100

(b) Pl. Bk. vol. 15, p. 4; 6 Jan. 1773; in Craven Co., north side of Tyger River on waters of Beaver Dam Branch; bd'd John White, vacant land; sur. 1 Sept. 1773.

(c) Union, Spartanburg.

327. FRANCIS ARTHBUTHNET 450

(This appears to be a duplication of No. 270)

328. JEAN MOUNCY 100

329. ROBERT SPENCE 100

(b) P.F. 1774; 6 Jan. 1773; on waters of Cuffee Town, 96 Dist.; bd'd William Walker, Isabell Walker, John Hamilton; sur. 11 May 1773.

(c) Edgefield.

330. JEAN SPENCE 100

(b) P.F. 1773; 5 Jan. 1773; in 96 Dist., Granville Co.; bd'd Robert Spence, Samuel Halladay, Mr. McIntosh, Francis Walker, Thos. Walker; sur. 11 May 1773.

(c) Newberry.

331. JAMES BLAIR 350

Possibly survey under No. 28 **(Lord Dunluce)** belongs to this James Blair.

332. WILLIAM WINBECK 100

(b) P.F. 2038; 6 Jan. 1773; on northeast side of Saludy on branch called Little River; bd'd Thos. Addamson, Rich'd Win, John Bowie; sur. 12 April 1775.

(c) Newberry, Laurens.

333. JOHN LOUGNECK 100

(b) P.F. 1135; 6 Jan. 1773; in Craven Co., Camden Dist.; bd'd John Blean; sur. 21 March 1773.

(c) Kershaw.

Ordered that the Secretary do prepare warrants of survey as prayed for by the several petitioners.

* * * *

SOUTH CAROLINA, 6 January 1773

It is ordered by his Excellency, the Governour, that the Secretary do prepare warrants of survey for the undermentioned persons.

334. TIMOTHY McLINTO 500

(b) Pl. Bk. 18, p. 294; 11 Dec. 1772, to Timothy McClintok, 250 acres in Craven Co. on waters of Fishing Creek; bd'd Jno. and Wm. Knox, Abraham Wright, Widow McClure, Wm. McClure, Widow Hannah, Widow Englis, vacant land; cert. 11 April 1773.

(c) Chester, York.

(d) He signed the above mentioned letter as "Timothy McClintock"; possibly search of will and deed books under that spelling would be productive.

335. JOSEPH LOWREY 150

(b) P.F. 1142; 11 Dec. 1772; in Craven Co. on branch of Wateree; bd'd Patrick Lowery, vacant land; sur. 1 Jan. 1773.

(d) He signed the above mentioned letter.

336. NATHAN BROWN 300

(b) P.F. 213; 11 Dec. 1772; in fork of Broad and Saludy Rivers, in Berkeley Co., on Hendricks Branch of south fork of Dunkins Creek; bd'd Wm. Scott, Moses Strickland, Wm. Hendricks, John Moore; sur. 2 Feb. 1773.

(c) Laurens.

(d) He signed the above mentioned letter.

337. JOHN PEDON 150

(b) P.F. 1482; 11 Dec. 1772; to John Pedan; in Craven Co. on branch called Fargeson Creek, waters of Tiger River; bd'd James Pedan, Thomas Pedan, "by old lines," vacant land; sur. 18 Jan. 1773.

(c) Spartanburg; Chester.

(d) He signed the above mentioned letter as "John Peddan." The Pension (S-30649) of Samuel Peden (360) stated John had sons John, James, Thomas, William, Samuel, Alexander and David, and daughters, Janet, Elizabeth and Mary; see Nos. 357, 341, 361a, 358, 360, 359, 408, and 361. The son Thomas is probably the Thomas mentioned in the survey as having land bordering that surveyed for John. This land was surveyed in 1768 for Thomas Pedan. It therefore appears that the son Thomas had preceded the rest of the family.

Howe [8] states these Pedans were children of John Peden and Peggy McDill, that John had been a ruling elder in the church in Ireland; that he settled first in Spartanburg, but during the Revolution he and his wife and younger members of the family "refuged" to Chester Co., where he died, but that most of his children settled around Fairview Church, on the waters of Reedy River in District of Greenville. However, records indicate several of them took up their original surveys in Fairfield or Chester.

338. JOHN BROWN 350

(b) P.F. 211; 11 Dec. 1772; in Craven Co., on north side of north fork of Tiger River; bd'd Samuel Snoddy; sur. 19 Jan. 1773.

(c) Spartanburg.

339. ALEXANDER BROWN 100

(b) P.F. 202; 11 Dec. 1772; in Craven Co., on branch of Wards Creek, branch of Tiger River; bd'd Andrew Cowen, vacant land; sur. 15 March 1773.

(c) Spartanburg, Union.

(d) He signed the above mentioned letter as "Alex. Brown."

340. JAMES STINSON 200

(b) P.F. 1800; 11 Dec. 1772; in Craven Co., branch of Rocky Creek; bd'd William Hickling, James Strong, Gasper Sliker, Samuel Maxwell; sur. 8 March 1773.

(c) Chester.

(d) He signed the above mentioned letter. According to family records of his age, he was born in Ireland about 1746, and married in Ireland Nellie (Ellaner, Ellen) whose maiden name is not known.

---

[8] George Howe, History of the Presbyterian Church in South Carolina, pp. 546-547.

Their children were Hugh, born in Ireland 1766, a daughter who died on the way to America and was buried at sea, Margaret, born Nov. 28, 1770 in Ireland, John, born in Ireland in 1772, Mary Ann, born in South Carolina in 1774, Robert, born 1776, William born 1778, Rebecca born 1781, the four last mentioned all in South Carolina. James Stephenson (under the spelling of "Stinson" in most records) served in the Revolution and was in the engagement at Kings Mountain. The daughter Margaret (born 1770) married her cousin Hugh W. Stephenson, son of No. 362 William Stinson (Stephenson). Some information is available as to the descendants of James and Nellie, but a complete record of decendants is yet to be compiled.

341. JAMES PEDEN 300

(b) P.F. 1483; 11 Dec. 1772; in Craven Co. on branch of Forgisen Creek, waters of Tiger River; bd'd vacant land; sur. 13 Jan. 1773.

(c) Spartanburg, Union.

(d) He signed the above mentioned letter "James Peddan."

342. JOHN MONTGOMERY 300

(b) P.F. 1338; 11 Dec. 1772; in Granville Co., on branch of Long Cane known by the name of Calhoun Creek; bd'd Thomas Bell, John Crain, vacant land; sur. 22 Feb. 1773.

(c) Abbeville.

(d) He signed the above mentioned letter.

343. JAMES HOOD 250

(b) While no survey was found for him (some have been lost or destroyed) it is known he took up or bought land in what was later Fairfield, through reference to his land as boundary or corners to land of others. See also 292.

(c) Fairfield.

(d) He signed the above mentioned letter.

344. JOHN McLINTO 400

(d) He signed the above mentioned letter as "John McClintock." Probably a search under that name would result in identifying his land and place of settlement.

345. THOMAS McDILL 400

(b) P.F. 1186; 11 Dec. 1772; in Craven Co., on branch of Rocky Creek; bd'd by Walter Brown, Robert Wiley, Widow Adam, ——— Mathews, William Mophet, David Chesnut; sur. 14 Jan. 1773.

(c) Possibly Abbeville.

(d) See National Genealogical Society Quarterly, June 1944, p. 44. He signed the above mentioned letter.

346. SAMUEL KERR 150

(b) P.F. 1023; 11 Dec. 1772; on north side Cedar Creek, a branch of Wateree River; bd'd Andrew Nutt; vacant land; sur. 2 Jan. 1773.

(c) Lancaster.

(d) He signed the above mentioned letter.

347. ROBERT MCLINTO 100

(b) Pl. Bk. vol. 18, p. 293; 11 Dec. 1772; to Robert McClentok (but indexed McLinto); in Craven Co., south side of Enaree River on Pattersons Branch of Indian Creek; bd'd John Were; vacant land; sur. 8 Jan. 1773.

(c) Newberry, Laurens.

(d) He signed the above mentioned letter as "Rev'd Robt. McClintock."

348. WILLIAM MCLINTO 100

(b) Pl. Bk. vol. 18, p. 296; to William McLento; on Little River on north side Broad River, Craven Co.; bd'd Joseph Lord, John Nagwares, vacant land; sur. 1 March 1773.

(c) Fairfield.

349. PATRICK LOWREY 100

(b) P.F. 1142; 11 Dec. 1772; in Craven Co., on waters of Wateree Creek; bd'd Joseph Lowry; sur. 7 Feb. 1773.

(c) Fairfield or Kershaw, Richland, Sumter.

350. JAMES BROWN 200

(b) Possibly Royal Grants, vol. 32, p. 514; in Berkley Co., Amelia Township on branch of Lions Creek; bd'd Frederick Smith, Charles Russell; Adam Miller, Jacob Powell; George Reddy; cert. by Surveyor General 4 May 1773; grant dated 31 Aug. 1774.

351. ROBERT BROWN 100

(b) P.F. 214; 11 Dec. 1772; on south side Broad River, on Gilders Creek, Barkley Co.; bd'd Wm. Young, Jas Burns, Alexander Kennedy, vacant land; sur. 6 Jan. 1773.

(c) Newberry.

325. JANET GIBSON 100

(b) P.F. 680; 11 Dec. 1772; in Berkley Co., in Fork of Siludy and Broad Rivers, on branch of Kings Creek; bd'd Thomas Dugan, ——— Gilders, ——— Willcock, vacant land; sur. 3 Jan. 1773.

(c) Newberry.

353. MARGARET PATON 100

354. JANE JOHNSTON 100

(b) P.F. 973; 11 Dec. 1772; in Fork of Broad and Siludy Rivers, on a branch of Gilders Creek, Barkley Co.; bd'd William Young, Robert Brown, ——— Kenady, Wm. Tiney, vacant land; sur. 6 Jan. 1773.

(c) Newberry.

355. JOHN CALWELL 250

(b) P.F. 262; 11 Dec. 1772; in Craven Co., in fork of Tiger River;

bd'd Middle Fork, North Fork, Elaxander Booyey, Elizabeth Pedan; sur. 16 Jan. 1773.

(c) Spartanburg.

(d) He signed the above mentioned letter as "John Caldwell."

356. ANDREW COWAN 100

(b) P.F. 371; 11 Dec. 1772; in Craven Co., on small branch of Wards Creek, waters of Tiger River; bd'd William Peden, vacant land, sur. 15 March 1773.

(c) Spartanburg, Union.

357. JOHN PEDEN 100

(b) P.F. 1483; 11 Dec. 1772; in Craven Co., on small branch called Mills Creek; bd'd vacant land; sur. 28 May 1773.

(c) Fairfield.

(d) Son of 337 John, which see.

358. SAMUEL PEDEN 100

(b) P.F. 1483; 11 Dec. 1772; in Craven Co., on small branch, waters of Enoree River; bd'd Herman Dildinas, vacant land; sur. 16 April 1773.

(c) Spartanburg, Union, Newberry.

(d) Samuel Peden applied in 1833 for a pension (S-30649) from the United States for his service in the Revolution. The application furnished information as to his parents, brothers and sisters (for abstract of which see 337, John Peden) and also some data on his career. He was born in Ireland in 1754, volunteered in Spartanburg Dist., S. C., October 1775 under Capt. Andrew Berry, served in the Snow Campaign, and gives details of subsequent service all over South Carolina, including Kings Mountain. In his brother Alexander's pension he is referred to as "Captain" Samuel. He stated that after the war he lived three years in North Carolina, then until 1818 in South Carolina in which year he went to Alabama. In 1833 he was in Fayette Co., Ala. On 20 December 1834 he was of Kemper Co., Miss. He was granted the pension, certificate being sent 1 May 1836. But as of 6 January 1836 Samuel Peden of Fayette Co., Ala., wrote that Samuel Peden, the applicant, had died on 26 December 1835. And on 4 April 1836 Margaret Peden of Kemper Co., Miss., reported her husband had died 26 December 1835.

359. DAVID PEDEN 100

(b) P.F. 1483; 11 Dec. 1772; in Craven Co., on small branch, waters of Enaree River; bd'd Samuel Peden, vacant land; sur. 24 April 1773.

(c) Spartanburg, Union, Newberry, Laurens.

(d) Son of John Peden, No. 337, which see.

360. ALEX'R PEDEN 100

(b) P.F. 1483; 11 Dec. 1772; in Craven Co. on Wards Branch, waters of Tiger River; bd'd ——— Curry, vacant land; sur. 18 Jan. 1773.

(c) Spartanburg.

(d) He served in the Revolution. His pension application (S-21417) states he was born in Ireland in 1756, came to America when 16, lived in Greenville District when he enlisted in 1775, and gives details of his service up to and including 1781. He lived in South Carolina after the Revolution. As his pension was paid up to 21 January 1841, that was probably the date of his death.

361. ELIZ'TH PEDEN 100

(b) P.F. 1483; 2 Dec. 1772; in Craven Co., on north fork of Tiger River; bd'd by river, John Colwell, vacant land; sur. 16 Jan. 1773.

(c) Spartanburg.

361 (a). WILLIAM PEDEN ....

His name is not listed among those to whom warrants for survey were authorized in the Council Journal. Nevertheless, one was issued on the same date as those of his father (No. 337) and his brothers and sisters. The survey was made and the land granted to him in due course. Apparently in copying the long list of Pedens into the Council Journal his name was omitted inadvertently, for the precept was dated the same day as those of the other members of the family.

(b) P.F. 1483; 11 Dec. 1772; 100 acres in Craven Co., on Wards Branch, waters of Tiger River; bd'd Currey, vacant; sur. 18 Jan. 1773.

(c) Union, Spartanburg.

362. WILLIAM STINSON 100

(b) P.F. 1800, 11 Dec. 1772; in Craven Co., on branch of Rocky Creek; bd'd "land laid out for the dutch," Charles Dick; sur. 9 April 1773.

(c) Chester.

(d) Chester Co. Deed Bk. O, p. 468; 3 July 1793; William Stinson, planter, of Chester Co., and wife Elizabeth sells to Francis Elliot, planter, 100 acres (as described in the survey) signed "Wm. Steenson," Elizabeth Stenson, her mark."

Before this time, in fact prior to the Revolution he had moved from Chester to York Co., and settled in the vicinity of Kings Mountain.

This William Stephenson was born in Ireland in 1744. He married first, in 1764, in Ireland a Miss Beattie (first name illegible on records). They had seven children: Hugh W., born January 25, 1765; John, Robert, James and William were all born in Ireland. Twin girls, Elizabeth and Nancy, were born in 1787 in South Carolina. His wife died the day the twins were born. In 1789 he married Elizabeth Wylie, who had come with her parents to South Carolina after the Revolution. By the second marriage there were four children: Samuel, born 1790, Mary, born 1792, Daniel Green, 1794, Catherine, 1796.

He died in 1809. His second wife died in 1811. He is buried between his two wives in the Old Burnt Church Cemetery in Chester Co.

He kept a store and operated a still, making frequent trips to Charleston for supplies. Quite a bit is known about him, as his son Daniel Green Stinson, who was a prolific writer, prepared an account of him for Dr. Lyman Draper and others from materials he had collected for histories of Sumter, Kings Mountain, and the Presbyterian Church. Some of this material was published by Howe in his account of the church, by Mrs. Ellet in her **Domestic History of the Revolution** and other works, and by Dr. Draper, as well as local newspapers, but much of it is still unused in the Draper papers. His son Hugh W. married his cousin Margaret Stephenson (see No. 340). They were the grandparents who reared John Calvin Stephenson, and taught him to carry on the family traditions. In the early 20th Century, when he was about 80 years of age, he compiled a detailed account of the descendants of his grandparents and included many of those descended from his great-grandparents William and James. While lacking in dates it gives relationships and places of residence and forms the basis for a complete account of this family.

363. MARGARET MONTGOMERY 100

(b) P.F. 1369; 11 Dec. 1772, in Granville Co., waters of Calhouns Creek; bd'd James Petigrew, Senr., James Petigrew, Jr., Roger McKinney, Jr., John Lackie, vacant land; cert. 3 June 1773.

(c) Abbeville.

364. JOHN KIRK 100

(b) P.F. 1040; 11 Dec. 1772; in Colleton Co., on northwest fork of Long Cane; bd'd John Tynes, Andrew McAlaster, John Hunt, vacant land; sur. 25 March 1773.

(c) Abbeville.

365. JOHN PARKER 300

He signed the above mentioned letter.

366. ROBERT WILSON 100

He signed the above mentioned letter.

367. JAMES WILSON 100

(b) P.F. 2024; 11 Dec. 1772; in Granville Co., waters of Calhoun Creek; bd'd Bartholomew Cropman, John Montgomery; sur. 1 Mar. 1773.

(c) Abbeville.

(d) Possibly the testator Abbeville Wills, vol. 1, p. 594; James Wilson, 13 March 1812; Daughters: Elizabeth McCracken, Mary Robinson, Nancy Wilson; son William, son James Henry, now a minor.

368. JOHN BETTY 300

(b) P.F. 124; 11 Dec. 1772; in Long Cane settlement, 96 Dist.;

bd'd Jacob Langeles, Marie Magdalan Bellot, Jean Dupuy, Crawford's old place, Thos. Lynde, vacant land; sur. 6 Feb. 1773.

(c) Abbeville.

(d) This is possibly the John Betty (Beattie) who was an elder in the church in Ballymoney. It was probably his sister who was the first wife of William Stephenson (No. 362).

369. ROBERT HOOD 100

(b) P.F. 880; 11 Dec. 1772; in Craven Co., branch of Little River of Saludy called Mudlick; bd'd Thomas North, William Williamson, Richard North; sur. 30 May 1773.

(c) Laurens, Newberry.

(d) Possibly testator, Laurens Will Bk. 1-A, p. 120: Robert Hood, 20 August 1790; wife Jane, grandfather Kelly Cunningham, son Thomas, daughter Jenny Cunningham.

370. ELIZ'TH HOOD 100

(b) P.F. 880; 11 Dec. 1772; in Craven Co., on waters of Raburns Creek; bd'd James McClinto; sur. 30 Dec. 1772.

(c) Laurens.

371. JOAN HOOD 100

(b) P.F. 880; 11 Dec. 1772; to Jean Hood; in Ninety-Six Dist., on small branch of Bullocks Fork of Thicketty; bd'd John Boyes, vacant land; sur. 13 May 1773.

(c) York.

372. WILL'M ELSAR 100

(b) Pl. Bk. 15, p. 55; 11 Dec. 1772; 200 acres in Craven Co. on Reedy River; bd'd James Reyan, John Bow, others—names unknown; cert. 13 March 1773.

(c)

(d) He signed the above mentioned letter as "Wm. Eashler." (Perhaps his land could be identified under that spelling.)

373. ROBERT HASPEN 400

374. ALEXANDER CHEANY 100

(b) Pl. Bk. vol. 14, p. 71; 11 Dec. 1772; to Alexander Chesny; in Colleton Co., a branch of Pacolet, Broad River; bd'd Thomas Coacks, John Grendel, Robert Chesney (sic.), James Coacks; sur. 2 June 1773.

(c) Spartanburg, Union.

(d) This is the son of Robert Chesney who bought his land so does not appear in the lists but signed the above mentioned letter as "Robt. Machesney." Alexander was subsequently a well-known Loyalist, and after the war returned to Ireland. His "journal," published in 1921, furnished some details of the quarantine; see Chapter 3.

375. ANN HASNEY 100

376. JOHN SNODDY 300

(b) P.F. 1764; 11 Dec. 1772; in Craven Co., on small branch called The Mill Creek, waters of Tiger River; bd'd vacant land; sur. 9 Jan. 1773.

(c) Spartanburg, Union.

(d) He signed the above mentioned letter as "John Snody."

377. MARY SNODDY 100

(b) P.F. 1764; 11 Dec. 1772; in Craven Co., on small branch of waters of Tiger River; bd'd James Edmondson, "old lines," vacant land; sur. 17 Jan. 1773.

(c) Spartanburg, Union.

378. SAMUEL SNODDY 100

(b) P.F. 1764; 2 Dec. 1773; in Craven Co., on north side of north fork of Tiger River; bd'd river, John Brown, vacant; cert. 9 Jan. 1773.

(c) Spartanburg.

(d) Probably testator Spartanburg Will Bk. 1-A-98; Samuel Snoddy, 6 April 1817, pr. 9 June 1817; wife; sons: John, Isaac, Andrew, Samuel, Alexander.

379. THOMAS DUNLAP 100

(b) P.F. 505; 11 Dec. 1772; in Barkley Co. in fork between Broad River and Saludy, on small branch of Tyger River called Pounding Mill Branch; bd'd William Smith, Robert Condon; sur. 19 Jan. 1773.

(c) Spartanburg, Union.

380. ROBERT HADIN 150

(b) P.F. 678; 11 Dec. 1772; to Robert Hadden; in Colleton Co., on small branch of northwest fork of Long Cane; bd'd William Ellis, vacant land; sur. 10 Feb. 1773.

(c) Abbeville.

(d) He signed the above mentioned letter as "Robert Hadden."

381. WILLIAM BOYD 250

(b) P.F. 170; 11 Dec. 1772 (Pl. Bk. 13, p. 328, 5 Dec. 1772); in Berkely Co., in fork between Broad and Saluda, on branch of Patterson Creek called Scott Branch; waters of Enoree River; bd'd William Proctor, John Kennedy, vacant lands, Mr. Robert McClento, James Proctor, Alexander Turner, John Armstrong, William Scott (Pl. Bk. substitutes Robert McCants for Mr. Robert McClinto, and Alexander Furman for Alexander Turner).

(c) Newberry.

(d) Chester Co. Wills, vol. 1, Bk. B, p. 25, will of William Boyd of Chester Co. 2 June 1800, pr. August 1800; son Alexander; eldest daughter Mary Boyd 100 acres of the 250 acres in Newberry; and daughter Martha Boyd, her sons William and Robert Boyd, her daughter Mary:

youngest daughter Jennet Keedey, her son William Keedey; wit.: John Keedey, etc.

He signed the above mentioned letter.

382. JOHN THOMSON 100

(b) P.F. 1867; 11 Dec. 1772; in Craven Co.; bd'd William Williamson; vacant land, on waters of Turkey Creek; sur. 17 Feb. 1773.

383. THOMAS MCKEE 200

(b) P.F. 1209; 11 Dec. 1772, in Colleton Co., Boonsborrow Township; bd'd vacant land; sur. 23 Jan. 1773.

(Another Thomas McKee (No. 412) also came on this ship, and was also entitled to 200 acres. The above survey was for one of them, but which is not known.)

(c) Abbeville.

(d) May be testator, Abbeville Wills Bk. 1, p. 208; Thomas McKee; 20 Oct. 1796, pr. 26 March 1798; wife Martha; daughter Jean; sons Thomas, William, John, James, refers to unmarried children. He signed the above mentioned letter as "Thos. Makee."

384. WILLIAM ANDERSON 150

(b) P.F. 35; 11 Dec. 1772; in Craven Co. on branch of Singletons Creek; bd'd William Marshall, ——— Snow, vacant land; sur. 1 Feb. 1773.

(c) Kershaw, Chester.

(d) William Anderson married in 1772 in Ireland Nancy Stephenson, born in Ireland 1750, sister of James and William Stephenson (Stinson). He was killed at King's Mountain, leaving sons Robert and William and a daughter Mary, born 1774 who married Joshua Smith in South Carolina, and moved to Tennessee. His widow married second Daniel Green.

An account of Nancy (Stephenson) Anderson appeared in Mrs. Ellet's Women of the American Revolution (vol. 3), information being furnished by Daniel Green Stinson (son of her brother William Stephenson (Stinson), see No. 362. William Anderson signed the above mentioned letter.

385. JAMES MCLINTO 100

(b) P.F. 1226; 11 Dec. 1772; in Craven Co. on waters of Raburns Creek; bd'd Joseph Babb, William Burris, Elizabeth Hood, vacant land; sur. 29 Dec. 1772.

(c) Laurens.

386. WILLIAM SIMPSON 200

(b) P.F. 1721; 11 Dec. 1772; in Craven Co., on waters of Little River; bd'd Jacob Jones, Elizabeth Caldwell, vacant land; sur. 9 Feb. 1773.

(c) Fairfield, Laurens, Newberry.

(d) He signed the above mentioned letter.

387. ALEXANDER SIMPSON 100

388. ROBERT SIMPSON 100

(b) P.F. 1720; 11 Dec. 1772; in Craven Co. on waters of Bush River; bd'd Silvanus Walker; vacant land; sur. 30 May 1773.

(c) Laurens, Newberry.

389. JAMES SIMPSON 100

(b) P.F. 1717; 11 Dec. 1772; in Craven Co. on waters of Warriors Creek; bd'd vacant land, old surveys; sur. 14 Jan. 1773.

(c) Laurens.

390. PETER WYLLY 150

(b) P.F. 2076; 11 Dec. 1772; to Peter Wyley; in Craven Co. waters of Fishing Creek; bd'd William Taler, Jas. Farginson, Robert McFadin, John Wiley, John Downy; sur. 9 Jan. 1773.

(c) Chester, York.

(d) He signed the above mentioned letter as "Peter Willey."

391. ROSEY WYLLY 100

(b) P.F. 2076; 11 Dec. 1772; to Rose Wyley; in Craven Co., on waters of Fishing Creek; bd'd Samuel Kilwell, William Farginson, John Wyly; sur. 1 Jan. 1773.

(c) Chester, York.

392. ELIZABETH McCROY 100

393. WILLIAM ERVING 100

(b) Pl. Bk. vol. 15, p. 72; 11 Dec. 1772; to Wm. Ewing; on north side Broad River, on branch of Little River; bd'd John Thompson, vacant land; sur. 9 Feb. 1773.

(c) Fairfield, Chester.

394. CHARLES MILLER 150

(b) P.F. 1301; 11 Dec. 1772; in Craven Co. on branch of Rocky Creek; bd'd vacant land; sur. 5 Jan. 1773.

(c) Chester.

(d) He signed the above mentioned letter.

395. ROBERT NEIL 100

(b) P.F. 1393; 11 Dec. 1772; in Belfast Twp., 96 Dist.; bd'd vacant land; sur. 5 Feb. 1773.

(c) Abbeville.

(d) He signed the above mentioned letter as "Robt. Neile."

396. JOHN THOMSON 100

(b) P.F. 1867; 6 Jan. 1773; in Craven Co., north side of Tyger River, on waters of Cane Creek; bd'd Agnes Elliott, vacant lands; sur. 2 Sept. 1773.

(c) Union, Spartanburg.

(d) He signed the above mentioned letter as "John Thompson."

397. CHARLES BARBER 200

(b) P.F. 73; 11 Dec. 1772; in Craven Co. Camden Dist.; south side Wateree River on Milstone Creek; bd'd George Summers, David Miller; sur. 7 Jan. 1773.

(c) Kershaw.

(d) Probably testator Kershaw Wills, vol. 2, Bk. G, p. 10; Charles Barber, 23 Aug. 1810; wife Peggy; grandchildren Arthur B. Edwards and Diana Edwards; son-in-law George Marlor; cousin Charles Barber, son of Robert Barber, senior; Charles Barber Howel, son of Eps Howel (under age), son Nathaniel, Charles B. Marlor and Pegey Marlor.

398. JOHN DICKEY 150

(b) P.F. 457; 11 Dec. 1772; in fork of Siludy and Broad, on Kelleys Creek of Anoree in Barkeley Co.; bd'd Daniel Hasey, Alexander Dickey, Joseph Fish; sur. 9 Jan. 1773.

(c) Laurens, Newberry.

(d) He signed the above mentioned letter as "John Dicky."

399. ALEXANDER DICKEY 100

(b) P.F. 456; 11 Dec. 1772; in forks of Broad and Saluda Rivers on waters of Enoree, on Kelleys Creek; bd'd Criston Graber, John Boid, Fit (?) Beninger, Joseph Fish, John Dickey, David Hasey; sur. 9 Feb. 1773.

(c) Laurens, Newberry.

400. JANE DICKEY 100

(b) P.F. 457; 11 Dec. 1772; in Craven Co., between Broad and Saluda Rivers; bd'd Paul Williams, Daniel Horsey; sur. 8 March 1773.

(c) Laurens, Newberry.

401. JOHN DICKEY 100

(b) P.F. 457; 11 Dec. 1772; on south side Broad River, on south fork of Dunkings Crick, in Barkley Co.; bd'd Nathan Brown, Rubin Flenigan, vacant land; sur. 2 Feb. 1773.

(c) Laurens, Newberry.

402. ROBERT ROSS 200

(b) P.F. 1624; 11 Dec. 1772; 115 acres, part of a 200 acres warrant, in Long Cane, in Ninety-six Dist.; bd'd S. Edward, James McFaron, ——— Jones, Pat Calhown, Joseph Holms, Wm. Gervais; sur. 28 April 1773.

Also P.F. 1624; 11 Dec. 1772; 70 acres, part of a 200 acre warrant near Long Cane Mill in 96 Dist.; bd'd by prior survey, James Faron, Thos. Crasswell, Benj. Watson, Pat. Calhoun, Sr., Pat. Calhoun, Jr.; cert. 11 Feb. 1773.

(c) Abbeville.

(d) He signed the above mentioned letter. Probably testator, Abbeville Wills, vol. 1, p. 60; Robert Ross 12 July 1790, pr. 5 Oct. 1790; wife; grandchildren Robert and James McBride (under age); "if daughter Martha have more children they to share it," son-in-law Hugh McBride; ex. James McBride.

403. HANNAH BETTY 100

(b) P.F. 124; 11 Dec. 1772; in Long Cane, 96 District; bd'd Moses Bradford, Samuel Dickson, John Lewis Gervais, vacant land; cert. 11 Mar. 1773.

(c) Abbeville.

404. HUGH FORD 200

(b) P.F. 604; 11 Dec. 1772; in Barkley Co., in forks between Broad and Saludy Rivers, on small branch of Dunkins Creek called Crareys branch; bd'd by Thomas McCrary, Robert Roseburrow, vacant land; sur. 6 Jan. 1773.

(c) Laurens, Newberry.

405. HUGH LOGAN 100

(b) P.F. 1126; 11 Dec. 1772; on north side Broad River, in forks of Little River in Camden Dist., bd'd Edward Wats, vacant land; sur. 13 Feb. 1773.

(c) Fairfield, Richland.

(d) He signed the above mentioned letter "Hugh Loggan."

406. DAVID THOMSON 250

(b) P.F. 1865; 11 Dec. 1772; 265 acres in Craven Co. on branch of Little River called Jacksons Creek; bd'd James Johnson, Margaret Martin, James Russell, John Shaw, Mr. Coneley, Jane Wilson, Mr. McMullins, Robert Nilles; sur. 2 Jan. 1773.

(c) Fairfield.

(d) He signed the above mentioned letter "David Thompson."

407. JOHN RICHEY, SENIOR 250

(b) Pl. Bk. 20, p. 121; 11 Dec. 1772; in Craven Co., northeast side Reyburns Creek, on branch called Reynolds Branch; bd'd William O'daniel, vacant land; sur. 16 Jan. 1773.

(c) Laurens.

(d) He signed the above mentioned letter "John Rickey."

408. JANET PEDEN 100

(b) P.F. 1483; 11 Dec. 1772; to Jennet Peden, in Craven Co., Camden Dist., on north side of Water Eye River on branch of Beaver Creek; bd'd John finloe; sur. 4 Jan. 1773.

(c) Kershaw.

(d) She was the daughter of John Peden (No. 337), which see.

409. MARY RICHEY 100

(b) Pl. Bk. vol. 20, p. 125; 11 Dec. 1772; on branch of Reyburns Creek called Jones Branch; bd'd vacant land; sur. 22 Jan. 1773.

(c) Laurens.

410. JOHN RICHEY, JUNIOR 100

(b) Pl. Bk. vol. 20, p. 122; 11 Dec. 1772; in Craven Co., south fork of Reyburns Creek; bd'd vacant land; sur. 16 Feb. 1773.

(c) Laurens.

411. ELEANOR RICHEY 100

(b) Pl. Bk. vol. 20, p. 122; 11 Dec. 1772; in Craven Co., Reyburns Creek, on branch thereof called Daniels Branch; bd'd Benj. Jones, William Daniel, vacant land; sur. 22 Jan. 1773.

(c) Laurens.

412. THOMAS MCKEE 200
(See No. 383.)

413. AGNES SIMPSON 100

(b) P.F. 1716; 11 Dec. 1772; on waters of Warriors Creek, bd'd Jonathon Downes, vacant land; "bounty survey"; sur. 14 Jan. 1773.

These (above persons) are poor people who have Sworn they are not worth £5 — Each —

* * * *

A List of the Passengers who arrived in this Province from Ireland in the Brigantine Free Mason and this Day petitioned for Land vizt.

414. JOHN RICHEY 100

(b) Pl. Bk. vol. 20, p. 123; 6 Jan. 1773; on north side Broad River, Craven Co., on branch of Hufmans Creek; bd'd John Winn, Alexander Turner, vacant land; sur. 25 July 1773.

415. JOHN MCKNIGHT 350

(b) P.F. 1221; 3 Jan. 1773; in Craven Co., on south side Broad River, and Surrats Creek; bd'd Robert Sn——— (?); sur. 25 May 1773.

(d) York Co. Wills vol. 1, p. 39, John McKnight, 20 June 1785, pr. 13 Feb. 1789; wife; son Robert; daughters; Mary, Sarah, Eleanor, Isabella, Betsy; refers to 100 acres in York Co. and 350 acres on Serats Creek in 96 Dist.

416. THOMAS MCLELLAND 100

417. SAMUEL PATERSON 350

(b) P.F. 1471; 6 Jan. 1773; in Hillsborough Twp., 96 Dist.; bd'd Nick'es Bonchillon, Jean Bellats, Jacob Delchaux, Mary Patterson, James Clark, Pat Calhoun; sur. 12 Feb. 1773.

(c) Abbeville.

(d) Probably testator, Abbeville Wills, old bk. 2, p. 167 (copy p. 132), Samuel Paterson, senior, farmer; 30 March 1821; pr. 8 Oct. 1824; wife Rachel; sons: John, Robert, Samuel; Jenny, wife of dec'd son Andrew and her daughters Betsy Baggs and Rachel; grandson Samuel, only son of dec'd son Samuel.

418. ROBERT NISBETT 400

(b) P.F. 1415; 6 Jan. 1773; in Craven Co., middle fork of Tyger River, chiefly on south side; bd'd ——— Sharp, Samuel Nisbett, James Wofford, Thomas Penny; sur. 24 Feb. 1773.

(c) Spartanburg.

419. JOHN PRESSLEY 300

(b) P.F. 1540; 6 Jan. 1773; in Granville Co. on Rocky Branch, waters of Long Cane Creek; bd'd Robert Neel, Samuel Presley, Mary Presley; sur. 8 March 1774.

(c) Abbeville.

(d) Possibly testator or father of testator Abbeville Wills, vol. 1, p. 522, John Presly, 6 Nov. 1808, pr. 20 March 1809; wife Nancy; "my child if she has one."

420. SAMUEL MCKAY 450

(Above persons) Able to pay

The undermentioned persons are not able to pay for their Warrants.

421. HENRY THOMSON 200

(b) P.F. 1866; 6 Jan. 1773; in Craven Co., south side Broad River, waters of Kings Creek; bd'd Jno. Steel, Jas Wilson, Jno. Brown, Thomas Crosson; sur. 25 Jan. 1773.

(c) Newberry.

422. WILLIAM THOMSON 100

(b) P.F. 1872; 6 Jan. 1773; in Craven Co., south side Broad River on branch of Kings Creek; bd'd John Steel, Jane Wilson, Jared Smith; sur. 25 Jan. 1773.

(c) Newberry.

423. ROBERT THOMSON 100

(b) Pl. Bk. 20, p. 235; 6 Jan. 1773; in Craven Co., north side Tiger River on Bever Dam Branch; bd'd vacant land; sur. 2 Sept. 1773.

(c) Spartanburg.

424. JOHN THOMSON 100

(b) P.F. 1869; 6 Jan. 1773; in Craven Co., north side of Tyger River, waters of Cane Creek; bd'd Agnes Elliott; sur. 2 Sept. 1773.

(c) Union, Spartanburg.

425. ISAAC LIVINGSTON 300

(b) P.F. 1121; 6 Jan. 1773; in .96 Dist. between Broad and Saluda

Rivers, on branch of Indian Creek, thence to Annore and Broad Rivers; bd'd Anesworth Middleton; sur. 18 Feb. 1773.

(c) Newberry.

426. JOHN MULLEN 100

427. JOHN BROWN 300

    (b) P.F. 211; 6 Jan. 1773; on Bever Creek in Parish of St. Marks, Craven Co., bd'd Mrs. Brownlow, John Ridd; vacant land; cert. 20 Feb. 1773.

428. EDWARD MCGREARY 100

    (b) P.F. 1202; 6 Jan. 1773; on branch of Great Flat Rock Creek, in Parish of St. Marks, Craven Co.; bd'd John Campbell, John Snow, Patrick Claton; sur. 16 March 1773.

429. JOHN RIDDLE 300

    (b) Pl. Bk. vol. 20, p. 108; 6 Jan. 1773; 100 acres on branch of White Oak Creek, northeast side of Wateree, Craven Co.; bd'd James Marlow, John Moor, Patrick McFadon, vacant land; sur. 25 June 1774.

    Also p. 109, 6 Jan. 1773; 200 acres on south side Grannys Quarter Creek, northeast side Wateree River, Craven Co.; bd'd David Jordan, Mr. Mathews, George Ganter, Mr. Mellon, Henry Maxwell, John Betty, George Dixon; sur. 21 June 1774.

(c) Kershaw.

430. JEAN BEARD 100

    (b) P.F. 95; 6 Jan. 1773; on mill creek of Turkey Creek on north side of Broad River; bd'd William Beard, vacant land; sur. 4 June 1773 (endorsed Jane Beard).

(c) York.

431. HUGH ANDERSON 100

    (b) P.F. 29; 6 Jan. 1773; in Colleton Co., on Cane Savannah branch about 2 miles above where Hance McCalloh now lives; sur. 10 May 1773.

(c) Edgefield.

432. ISABELLA FOSTER 100

    (b) P.F. 612; 6 Jan. 1773; in Long Cane settlement, in 96 Dist.; bd'd Mary Parkeson, John Anderson; sur. 1 March 1773.

(c) Abbeville.

433. JAMES FOSTER 100

    (b) P.F. 613; 6 Jan. 1773; in Granville Co., on waters of north fork of Long Caine; bd'd Charles Hamilton, Robert Cayton, Robert Campbell, Edward Fletcher; cert. 10 Feb. 1773.

434. WILLIAM FOSTER 300

    (b) Pl. Bk. 15, p. 195; 6 Jan. 1773; in settlement of Long Cane, Ninety-six Dist., bd'd Marie Magdalain Bellat, John Betty, Jacob Langel,

Thos. Lyndise, Township line of Hillsborough, Sarah Foster, Jean Bellat; cert. 9 March 1773.

(c) Abbeville.

435. SARAH FOSTER 100

(b) Pl. Bk. vol. 15, p. 194; 6 Jan. 1773; in Hillsborough Twp. in 96 Dist., bd'd William Foster, vacant land; cert. 10 March 1773.

(c) Abbeville.

436. ARTHUR McMACHON 100

(b) P.F. 1226; 6 Jan. 1773; to Arthur McMahon; on west side of Bever Creek in Parish of St. Marks, Craven Co.; bd'd John Brown and Mrs. Brownlow; sur. 2 April 1773.

437. CHARLES COAPLING 150

(b) P.F. 347; 6 Jan. 1773; in Craven Co., on waters of Samuel McMury Branch; bd'd Robert Elison; sur. 19 Feb. 1773.

438. ALEXAND COAPLING 100

(b) Pl. Bk. vol. 14, p. 185; 6 Jan. 1773; to Alexander Copland; on branch of Turkey Creek, north side Broad River, Craven Co.; bd'd William Minter, Charles Copland, John Richey; sur. 25 June 1773.

(c) Chester, York.

439. WILLIAM COAPLING, JUN'R. 100

(b) P.F. 347; 6 Jan. 1773; on forks of Jarratts Creek, south side of Broad River; sur. 6 April 1773.

440. JANE COAPLING 100

(b) P.F. 364; 6 Jan. 1773; to Jean Copeling; in Craven Co. on branch of Mill Creek; sur. 29 March 1773.

441. MARGARET BIGHAM 150

(b) Pl. Bk. vol. 13, p. 213; 6 Jan. 1773; in Craven Co., on Brushy Fork of Little River; bd'd vacant land; sur. 23 Feb. 1773.

(c) Fairfield, Richland or Newberry, Laurens.

442. WILLIAM COAPLING 350

(b) P.F. 347; 6 Jan. 1773; to William Coapland; on south side Broad River on Peoples Creek of Cherokee Creek, Colleton Co., bd'd vacant land; sur. 11 June 1773.

443. MARY McKNIGHT 100

(b) P.F. 1221; 3 Jan. 1773; Bartly Co., on ridge between Minnims(?) Creek and ——— a branch; bd'd vacant land; sur. 25 May 1773.

444. JANE McKNIGHT 100

(b) P.F. 1219; 6 Jan. 1773; in Craven Co., branch of Taylors Creek, south side Wateree River; bd'd Mikijah McDonald; sur. 20 Feb. 1773.

(c) York.

445. MARGARET MCKNIGHT 100

(b) P.F. 1221; 6 Jan. 1773; in Barckley Co., on Gilkeys Creek; bd'd David Luney, Loverick Bullock; 20 May 1773.

(c) York.

446. HUGH GORLEY 100

447. JAMES COX 300

(b) P.F. 374; 6 Jan. 1773; in Colleton Co., 96 Dist. on Dry Creek, a branch of Mine Creek, a water of Little Saluda; sur. 6 May 1773.

(c) Edgefield.

448. WILLIAM MCKEE 250

(b) P.F. 1210; 6 Jan. 1773; on branch of Grannys Quarter in Craven Co.; bd'd John Jasperfield; sur. 25 Feb. 1773.

(c) Kershaw.

449. JONATHON NISBETT 100

450. EMILA EGER 100

(b) Pl. Bk. vol. 14, p. 542; 6 Jan. 1773; to Amelia Eager; on branch of Hanging Rock Creek, in St. Mark's Parish, Craven Co.; bd'd Mrs. Love, Daniel Horton, vacant land; sur. 8 March 1773.

(c) Lancaster.

451. JOHN HALL 250

(b) P.F. 776; 1 Dec. 1773 [9] 200 acres in Craven Co., on waters of Enoree; bd'd Michael Walderips, Joseph Mowey (?), William Graghorn, vacant; sur. 15 Jan. 1773.

452. GEORGE BARNES 100

(b) P.F. 77; 6 Jan. 1773; in Charleston Dist., St. Georges Parish, in the fork of the four holes and The Wall Nut Creek; bd'd Sarah Caruthers; vacant land; sur. 6 May 1773.

(c) Orangeburg, Dorchester, Berkeley.

453. MARGARET BEARD 100

(b) P.F. 95; 6 Jan. 1773; in Craven Co., on branch of Turkey Creek called Mill Creek; bd'd Valentine Bell, vacant land; sur. 2 June 1773.

454. WILLIAM BEARD 100

(b) P.F. 96; 6 Jan. 1773, in Craven Co., north side of Broad River, on Mill Creek of Turkey Creek; bd'd Balantine Bell, Market Beard, vacant land; sur. 2 June 1773.

455. MARY PATTERSON 100

(b) P.F. 1468; 6 Jan. 1773; to Mary Paterson, in Hillsborough Twp., 96 Dist.; bd'd Jacob De Le Chaux, Samuel Patterson, Jean Bellat; sur. 12 Feb. 1773.

456. JOHN THURSDALE 250

(b) Memorials, vol. 2, p. 301; Craven Co., on branch of Lynches

[9] Obviously an error, as the survey was made 15 January 1773.

Creek; bd'd vacant land, cert. 30 Sept. 1774, granted 17 March 1775.

(c) Lancaster, Chesterfield, Kershaw, Darlington, Sumter.

457. JAMES WILSON 100

(b) P.F. 2030; 6 Jan. 1773; in Barkley Co., in fork between Broad and Saluda River on Ferguson Creek; bd'd John Patten, George Brewton, John McCorley; sur. 1 March 1773.

458. ANDREW TAYLOR 200

(b) P.F. 1841; 6 Jan. 1773; on Long Canes in 96 Dist.; bd'd Arch. McCleland, And'w Ross, Samuel Leard, Jane Hilles, John Wilson, John David; sur. 22 Feb. 1773.

(c) Abbeville.

459. MARY PRESLEY 100

(b) P.F. 1540; 6 Jan. 1773; in Colleton Co., on waters of Stephenson Creek; bd'd Samuel Presley, John Harse (?); sur. 21 Jan. 1773.

(c) Abbeville.

460. JAMES BREDEN 300

(b) Pl. Bk. vol. 13, p. 321; 6 Jan. 1773; 100 acres on branch of Wateree River, Craven Co.; bd'd James Moare, John Dougherty, John Lowry, John Buckannan, vacant land; sur. 19 March 1773.

Also, p. 322; 6 Jan. 1773, 200 acres on branch of White Oak Creek, northeast side of Waterce, Craven Co.; bd'd Widow Kirkland, John Kirkland, Francis Hodge, Robert Domiles (or Daniles), James McCullough; cert. 18 Mar. 1773.

(c) Fairfield, Kershaw.

461. CHA'S STUART 100

(b) P.F. 1816; 6 Jan. 1773; in Craven Co. on horse head branch; sur. 15 May 1773.

462. JOHN FLEMAN 100

(b) P.F. 591; 6 Jan. 1773; in Camden Dist., branch of Cedar Creek; bd'd Alexander Keniday.

(c) Lancaster.

463. WILLIAM SHANE 100

(b) P.F. 1694; 6 Jan. 1773; on head or upper branches of Little Lynches Creek; bd'd John Riddle; sur. 23 March 1773.

(c) Lancaster.

464. CHARLES COAPLING 100

(b) P.F. 364; 6 Jan. 1773; to Charles Copeling; in Craven Co., on branch of Turkey Creek; sur. 14 April 1773.

(c) Chester, York.

465. CATH'N STEVENSON 100

(b) P.F. 1794; 6 Jan. 1773; to Catherine Stevenson; on branch of

Mill Creek in north fork of Tyger River in Craven Co.; bd'd vacant land; sur. 25 May 1773.

(c) Spartanburg.

466. RICH'D MCCLURKAN 150

(b) P.F. 1169; 6 Jan. 1773; in Craven Co., on branch of Caney (?) Creek, waters of Tiger River; bd'd Charles Denem, Isaac Crow; sur. 5 Feb. 1773.

(c) Spartanburg, Union.

467. W'M REYNOLDS 450

(b) Possibly Pl. Bk. vol. 20, p. 76; 5 Jan. 1773; to William Reynoldson; in Granville Co. on waters of Norris Creek, a branch of Long Cane (across corner of plot "path to Calhoun's"); bd'd vacant land; sur. 1 April 1773.

(c) Abbeville.

468. MARGARET DANILLS 100

(b) Pl. Bk. 14, p. 307; 5 Jan. 1772; to Margaret Daniel; in Colleton Co. on waters of Stephenson Creek; bd'd Mary Presslys, Samuel Pressley, vacant land sur. 2 Jan. 1773.

(c) Abbeville.

Ordered that the Secretary prepare Warr'ts as prayed for by the several petitioners.

CHAPTER 5

IDENTIFICATION OF IMMIGRANTS FROM IRELAND

I

Between 1750 and 1775 there was an enormous influx into South Carolina of persons from Ireland. While a few were Irish Baptists, Irish Quakers, or members of the Church of Ireland, the majority were Presbyterians, holding to the tenets of the Church of Scotland, and most of them were from northern Ireland. Divided into the many sects of that church they included Reformed (Covenanter), Associate, Burgher, Anti-Burgher, Seceders, etc., but all were considered Presbyterian and usually grouped together as "Scotch-Irish." (Originally this term was Scots-Irish but it has been corrupted in the United States into Scotch-Irish, to the annoyance of those of the same blood abroad. They insist that "Scotch" is a drink; persons are properly referred to as "Scots" or "Scottish" and if from Ireland of Scottish origin may be termed "Scots-Irish." In Ireland the designation now is "Ulster Scot.")

As many persons of the same surname often had the same first name, it has been difficult to identify a known "first ancestor in this country" with a specific immigrant or his origin in Ireland.

However, while still requiring much detail work, with patience and analyzation of various types of records, in many cases it is not impossible, particularly for those coming after 1769.

Between 1750 and 1769 the majority of the immigrants from Ireland came under the "Bounty." [1] For the most part, names of those are not readily identified with the ship

---

[1] See pp. 6-9.

on which they came. Possibilities of such identification are now being studied.

However, for those arriving after expiration of the bounty, or in some instances earlier, by following carefully the procedure outlined in Section II below, the date of arrival and general locality in Ireland from whence the specific person came can usually be determined.

It may seem a tedious procedure, but "short-cuts" are NOT advisable.

II

For the purpose of illustration, it will be assumed that the line of descent has been traced *back* generation by generation to a man living in a specific county of South Carolina prior to 1820, and it is definitely proven that HE is the ancestor. Following is the procedure then to be followed.

(a) The first step is to see if such proven ancestor owned any land (the majority of persons did). If so, see how he acquired it. Was it by purchase, inheritance, grant, etc.? For this, careful search must be made in the records of the county in which he lived. If he owned more than one tract, look up all of them. This means checking the deed records of the county, not only to see if he bought it but to see whether when he sold it he stated in his deed how he acquired it. If he bought it, look at the deed by which he acquired it and see if he states the county of which he was resident at that time. If he was selling it, see if the deed states he bought it, if it was inherited or if it was a grant, etc. In the latter case, be sure to note what kind of a grant and when it was granted (date, Royal grant, State grant, etc. If it does not state, note any reference to date or surveys). If deeds give no information as to how he acquired it, look for wills, not only of his father but of his brothers, uncles, father-in-law, etc. If a deed shows he bought it and refers to him as being of some other county, follow the same procedure in that county. The object is to prove that specific person (who has been proven to be the father of the next generation in line of descent) is identical with the man to whom that specific piece of land was granted. If it is found that he secured it by

Royal grant the procedure outlined in the next paragraph is unnecessary.

However, if the net result is that he bought it, and no record is found of him in that county prior to purchase and the deed does not indicate any other county as his residence when he bought it, then, and then only should one go to the land grants at the South Carolina State Department of Archives and History. There, having first determined, from other information you have about him, his approximate age, list all grants (both pre-Revolutionary and post-Revolutionary) to a person of that name *after* the time when your man would have been approximately 21 years old. Then it will be necessary to examine each grant (and possibly the survey on which it was based), ascertain the location of the land covered by each grant and through the records of the county concerned see whether, if he later sells it, it can be proven that the person selling it is THE ancestor you are tracing or that such land can be proven to be in the possession in the next generation of the children of *your* ancestor. Many false pedigrees have resulted from the assumption, on finding a grant to one of the *name* of an ancestor, that the grantee is the specific person in whom you are interested. In such a case much more work is required to prove the identity of the grantee with the ancestor. This procedure should not be resorted to until all efforts to trace the ancestor to the *original grant to him* have been exhausted.

Assuming the first step has been successfully taken and that the ancestor has been proven to be identical with a man who received a grant of a specific tract of land and, further, that it was a Royal grant (i.e., made before the Revolution, since the procedure outlined is directed toward pre-Revolutionary settlers and hence the records of that period), next steps are as follows:

(1) Prepare a memorandum giving the following information: Name of grantee, statement that the document in which interested is a Royal grant, date of grant (if known or secured from Archives records), county in which located, and note of any natural features used in deeds, wills or grants to help with identification.

(2) Then in the South Carolina Department of Archives and History, see the Index of Royal grants, look up name of grantee and get the reference to the Grant Book; look at it and get the date of the survey on which it was based.

(3) From the Index to Pre-Revolutionary Plats (surveys) locate the survey in the Survey Book, and from it get the date of the warrant or precept. If not found in the survey book or the entry does not give the date of the warrant or precept, then look at the original survey for such date.

(4) Having the date of the warrant or precept, go to the *Council Journal* for that date and read it carefully to see whether in directing that the warrant for survey be issued, there is any indication of the ship on which the person to whom it is to be issued came into the colony. (Here it should be remembered that the ship is not necessarily named, but between 1769 and 1775 it usually was. Also, as a rule, all persons coming on a ship petitioned for their land at the same time. If the statement is merely "recently arrived from Ireland," the next step is to go to the newspapers as mentioned in the next paragraph, and by seeing which ships arrived in the preceding 30 days or so, and checking with the *Council Journals* to determine the ships which *are* mentioned, the ship NOT so named can usually be determined. (If in the *Council Journal* entry authorizing the survey the name of the man in whom you are interested is merely included in a group of names of obviously mixed origin, or without any identification, it is probable that he did *not* come with a group directly from Ireland. Tracing him then is more difficult and requires quite different procedure.)

(5) Having the name of the ship, the next step is to verify the date of arrival in South Carolina and the port from which she sailed by looking in the *South Carolina Gazette* (copies are available on microfilm in the South Carolina Archives and other libraries). Begin with the date of the Council meeting at which the petitions were made, and go *backward* until reference is found to the arrival of the ship, which is usually reported under the heading of "Marine News." Be sure to find an *arrival* date, as under that heading is also listed vessels in port and sailing. The report of arrival will show

the name of the master of the vessel and the port from which it sailed. (Remember there were often several vessels of the same name, some of which were in the "local trade," that is, going back and forth to the various islands of the West Indies, so keep looking for a vessel of the name in which you are interested from an Irish port, if, of course, the *Council Journal* indicated the settler had come from Ireland.)

As, naturally, the tendency was to sail from the nearest port, knowing the port of sailing limits considerably the area to be searched for the ancestor in Ireland, and makes it possible to have such searches made.

If the port of sailing was one of the north of Ireland ports (Belfast, Londonderry, Newry, Larne, or Portrush) there is now available a volume which will help to narrow the search still further.

After having found from the *Council Journal* the ship, and from the newspaper the date of arrival and port from which it sailed, if further search is planned, and the port of sailing is one of the ports mentioned in the preceding paragraph, it will be very helpful to read *Ulster Emigration to Colonial America, 1718-1775*[2]. It gives a good account of the background in Ireland, and in Chapter VII "Ports and Agents," and the accompanying map of Ulster on p. 106-107, indicates the general area from which ships sailing from the several ports drew their passengers. In having research done in Ireland this will help materially in determining the area in which searches should begin.

If it is planned to have research done in Ireland, it is suggested that before making arrangements for it, *Irish and Scotch-Irish Ancestral Research*[3] be read or at least scanned, particularly the chapters referring to northern Ireland which describe the Public Record Office there, Presbyterian records, and in general the suggestions of the author with respect to types of records available. This work does NOT give any genealogical data as such, but tells what records were origi-

---

[2] *Ulster Emigration to Colonial America, 1718-1755* by R. J. Dickson, 1966. See Chapter I, footnote 5 (p. 5).

[3] *Irish and Scotch-Irish Ancestral Research*, by Margaret Dickson Falley, Apt. T, 1500 Sheridan Road, Wilmette, Ill. 60091. Privately printed.

nally created, what has been preserved, and where such records may be located.

By careful study of these two books, not only will there be a better understanding of what can be done but also by arranging for specific searches the cost may be greatly reduced.

It should be remembered that during the period of the bounty (prior to 1769) there were ships agents in the south of Ireland also and as there were Presbyterians, Baptists and Quakers in the south of Ireland, it seems logical that some of the "poor protestants" coming under the bounty would have come from that area. But that is another story and tracing them requires a different procedure, which is still under study.

The searcher is advised, before looking in the indexes of this volume for a name in which interested, to read the following chapter.

CHAPTER 6

VARIATION IN SPELLING OF SURNAMES

I

In tracing a line of descent (or ascent) it is often forgotten that prior to a hundred and fifty years ago there was no standard for spelling; ours was a purely phonetic language. Words were spelled in any way that indicated to the writer the sound when spoken. And this was complicated by the fact that the same letters or combination of letters did not convey the same sound to all hearers.

Even now there are slight regional variances in pronunciation, but then Colonial America and especially the south was an area where many dialects met. Here one had not only variations of Germanic tongues and several French patois, but from the British Isles alone Cornish, Welsh, Lowland Scots, Gaelic, Erse, and many local English dialects. The person writing a name spelled it with the letters which to him indicated the sound he had heard pronounced. Thus, if the record was prepared by someone other than the person concerned the spelling might depend on the spelling that to the person writing it indicated the sound rather than that of the person saying it.

In looking for records of a person, it is well to pronounce the name as nearly as possible as it would have been pronounced prior to 1800 by the person hearing it and if it was supposedly written by him look for it under that spelling. Always remember the additional factor as to what the sound as pronounced may have meant to the person writing it. (The writer learned this the hard way. The family in which interested came to Texas in 1870; and had as far as they knew always spelled it "Neale." They were Presbyterians from Giles Co., Tenn. The line was traced back to a William who appeared there around 1809 and the earliest record found was a voters list on which he appeared as "Neill." As a number of the Presbyterians there were Irish who had come from South Carolina, it seems logical that he might have been one of that group. But he could not be found among them or back in South Carolina. Meanwhile it had been learned that the name was spelled by the Irish "Neill," by Scottish "Neil," by English "Neal" or "Neale." And on checking it was found that the Clerk handling the preparation of the voters list was one of the Irish group from South Carolina! In time, the line was traced and turned out to be English into Salem, Mass., as early as 1642, then New Jersey, then Philadelphia, then to Giles Co., Tenn. Years were lost in assuming from the spelling that he might have been one of the Irish group. So the name should be looked for under all spellings.)

Note not only the spelling, but note whether the record was such that the bearer of the name might have written it himself or whether some other person would probably have written it.

Even in cases where the bearer wrote it himself he may have written it differently from time to time. (Some branches of the Stephensons did.) There is said to be a will of a wealthy Colonial Virginian, educated in England, who wrote his will himself and spelled his name five different ways in the document. It has been suggested that as he owned land in six or seven counties, in some of which the majority of settlers were German, in other Gaelic Scots, others south England (Wales or Cornwall), etc., he deliberately spelled it so as to convey to each group the sound as they pronounced it. The story may be apocryphal but it illustrates the point!

II

In order to help the searcher who is unfamiliar with the variation in spelling of some of the more frequently used surnames among the Scots-Irish, some are listed below. Many of them are variations of the names of persons coming in the Rev. William Martin's party (listed in Chapter 4) but others frequently met are included.

No doubt there are many other variations of these names,

and of names not included, but it so happens that these are the
only ones noted by the present writer.

However, a word of caution may be advisable here. *Look*
under varied spellings, but remember that when the name is
spelled differently from the way the family usually spelled it,
proof is required that it is the same family, or the same man.
All Browns were not Brouns or vice versa! While Cowan
may indicate a McEwen, all McEwens were not Cowens.

III

SOME VARIATIONS FOUND IN THE RECORDS

In the case of Celtic names, a prefix may be used, either
"Mc," "Mac", or "O".

Adams, Addams, Ardam, Audam, Oddams, McAdams.

Agnew, Agnu, Annu.

Alexander. (The nickname being "Sandy," that form is
sometimes used, or even Sanders, or Saunders.)

Barber, Barbar, Barba, Barbee.

Barlo, Barlow.

Bailey, Bayley, Bally.

Beard, Baird, Bard, Baud, Boyd, Boid, Bird, Byrd.

Berkeley, Barkley, Barclay.

Beattie, Beatty, Batty, Betty.

Blear, Blair, Bleer.

Blaine, Blean.

Bredon, Breedon, Breddon, Bradin.

Browne, Brown, Broon, Broun, Broune.

Brian, Bryan, Brines, Brynes.

Bryson, Brison, Briason.

Burnet, Butnett, Burtnet.

Caldwell, Cauldwell, Calwell, Colwell, Callwell, Couldwel.

Campbell, Cambel, Cammel, Camel, Comble (and sometimes
confused with Gamble).

Carney, Kearney.

Carnahan, Karnahan.

Cheney, Cheany, Chaney, Chainey.

Clark, Clarke, Clerk, Clerck.

Coapling, Copeland, Copland, Coupland, Caplan.

Cochran, Cockran, Cokeran, Kochran.

Cork, Kork, Coark, Corock.

Cowan, Cowen, Coan, Cohen, Kowan, McKowen, McEwen.

Cox, Cocks, Cocke, Coke.

Craig, Crag, Krag.

Crawford, Craiford, Croufor.

Creighton, Crateton, Kreighton.

Daniel, Danel, Danyle.

Daragh, Darraugh, Darrow.

Dial, Dyal, Deal, Dill, Dale; see also McDill.

Douglas, Duglas, Douglase.

Eger, Ager, Eager.   (See also Meager.)

Eliot, Elliot, Elliott, Alliotte.

Ewell, Yuile, Ewert, Youart, Yuart.

Fairey, Fairy, Faris, Ferris.

Fear, Fair.

Fleming, Flemming, Fleeman, Fleman.

Ferguson, Fergesson, Forginson.

Ford, Foard, Foord, Forard.

Gamble, Gambell, Gammel (and sometimes appears as Campbell).

Gillespie, Galespie, Galespy, Gelasey, Gallespy.

Gorley, Gourley, Gurley, Gurly.

Greg, Gregg, Graig (and, rarely, Craig).

Grim, Grimbs, Grimes, Grumbs.

Hadin, Hayden, Hadden.

Hall, Halle, Holle.

Hearton, Heerton, Heaton (and sometimes Eaton)

Harberson, Harbison, Herbinson.

Hewie, Hughie.

Hicklen, Hickling.

Hove, Hauve, which sometimes, though seldom, becomes Harf and Harve, or even Hoff.

Humphrey, Humfrey, Umfrey.
And remember that often the "H" is not sounded at all.

Irving, Irvin, Irvine, Ervine, Erving, and even Erwin or Irwin.

Jamieson, Jimmeson, Jameson, Jimson.

Johnson, Johnston, Johnstone.

Kelly, Kelley, Caley, Cale.

Kerr, Karr, Carr.

Leach, Leech, Leitch.

Lidey, Ladey, Lady, Leadie.

Loughneck, Longnick, Luffnick.

Linn, Lynne, Lyne.

Martin, Martyn, Marton, Marston.

Mebane, Meabin, Mebbin, Mabane, Maybeen, Maybean, Mebin, McBean, McBane, MacBean. Remember that "Mac" and "Mc" are used interchangeably and may even be dropped entirely at times.

McAlister, McCalister, MacAllester, McClester, MacClester.

McCance, McCants, McChants, Machants, Machance.

McCauley, McCawley, McCowle, Coule (and sometimes Cooley).

McCee, McKee, MaKay, Maxey, Maxcy, Makee.

Machesney, Chesney.

MacClure, McLure.

McClurken, McLurken, McClarkan.

McCree, McCrea, McRea, McRae, McRee.

McCreight, McCrate.

McCullough, McCollough, McCullow.

McDill, McDeal, McDeel, McDowell, McDial, Madill, Madel.

McFerrin, McFaran, McFearrin.

McKay, see McCee.

McEwin, McKewn.

McCowan, McKown.

McClellan, McClelland, McLeland, McLellan, Maclellen.

McLin, McClin, McLean, Macklin, McLean.

McLinto, MaClintock.

MacMahon, McMachon.

McMurragh, McMurray, McMorrough, Morrow, Morry, Murray.

McNarra, McNarraw, McNarrough, McNarry, McNary, Menary.

McNeil, McNeill, McNeilly, Menelly.

McQuestion, McQuiston, McKisten, McCuiston.

Morrow, see McMurragh.

Neill, Neil, Neale, Neilly.

Nesbitt, Nisbet.

Paterson, Patison, Patterson and even Beterson.

Paton, Patten, Patern.

Parker, Packer, Paker.

Peden, Pedan, Peaden, Paden, Peddon.

Presley, Pressley, Presly, Preaslee.

Ray, Rea, see McCree.

Raymond, Reamon, Ramon.

Reynolds, Rennals.

Richie, Richey, Ritchie.

Rork, Roarke, Rourke, O'Rourke (and even McCrourk)

Scott, Scot, Scoot, Scoat.

Shepherd, Shepard, Sheppard.

Sinclair, St. Clair, Sinkler. (And has been found as Cinquelar.)

Sproul, Sproll, Sprall.

Stephenson, Stevenson, Stinson, Steenson. (This last is the way it was pronounced on the Scottish Border.)

Stuart, Stewart, Steward.

Tate, Teat.

Thomson, Thompson, Tomson.

Todd, Toad.

White, Whyte, Wight.
Wiley, Willey, Wylie, Wylly.
Winn, Win, Wynne.
Young, Yonge.

INDEX OF PERSONS

Barrenow, Isaac	75
Barret, James	66
Barrows, William	66
Bass, Isaac	55
Bayer, Peter	66
Beard, Elenar	55
Elizabeth, Mrs.	55
James	49
Jane	97
Jean	97
John 54, 55, 62, 70,	71
Margaret 62,	99
Market	99
William 97,	99
Beattie, also Betty, Miss ———	87
Beatty, William	28
Beck	2
Belk 55, 73,	75
Bell, Balentine	99
John	68
Thomas	84
Valentine	99
Zacaria	46
Bellat, Jean 98,	99
Marie Magdalain 89,	97
Bellats, Jean	95
Beninger, Fit(?)	93
Bennet, Moses	58
Berry, Capt. Andrew	86
Beterson, William	67
Betty (Beattie), Hannah	94
John 88, 89,	97
Biggams, John	45
Bigham, Margaret	98
Bione ———	80
Black, Anguish	55
Blair, Brice	35
James 35, 46,	82
Margaret	46
Martha	46
Price	54
Sarah	46
Thomas 50,	57
William	46
Blean, John	82
Blear, John	80
Boggs (Bogs), Thomas	50
Boid, John	93
Bole, Mr. ———	31
Bonchillon, Nick'es	95

Bonner, Jennet	59
John	59
Booth, Benj.	45
William	28
Booyey, Elaxander	86
Bow, John	89
Bowie, John	82
Box, Robert	47
Boyakim, Samuel	51
Boyd, Alexander	90
Catherine (McClurken)	43
James	43
John	76
Mary 58,	90
Martha	90
Robert	90
William 31, 47, 50, 70,	90
Boyes, John	89
Bradford, Andrew	56
David	56
James	56
John	56
Mary	56
Moses	94
Robert	56
William	56
Bradley, Hamilton	65
Brady, Alexander 26, 27, 31, 80,	83
Breden, James	100
Brewton, George	100
Brooks, Richard	48
Brown, Alexander 31,	83
Elizabeth	49
George	80
James 35, 43, 59,	85
John 31, 49, 68, 80, 83,	
90, 96, 97,	98
Judith	50
Mary	80
Molly, Mrs.	80
Nathan 31, 82,	93
Robert	85
S.	28
Walter	84
William 75,	80
Brownlee, Jane	74
Brownlow, Mrs. ——— 97,	98
Brynes, Charles	62
Bryson, William	67
Buckannan, John	100
Bull, Governor	9
Bullock, Loverick	99
Zack	43

Cowan, Cowen, Cowin,
   Alexander   45
   Andrew   83, 86
   Elizabeth   45
   Jane   45
   John   45
   Robert   45, 56, 58
Cowsers, John   77
   Richard   77
Cox, James   99
Craig, Alex'r   71
   James   58
   John   35, 45, 59, 64
   Margaret   64
   Mary   59
Craige, William   59
Crain, John   84
Crams, James   66
Crasswell, Thos.   93
Crawford, ——   89
   Agnes   51
   Isabella   51
   James   35, 51
   Margaret   51
   Mary   51
   William   35, 51
Crea, Peter   59
Creighton, Thomas   50
Crellman, Sarah   49
Crismas, Samuel   46
Cropman, Bartholomew 88
Cross, John   69
Crosson, Thomas   96
Crow, Isaac   101
Culbreath, Joseph   76
Cunningham, Jean   57
   Jenny   89
   Kelly   89
   Patrick   48, 60
   Robert   76
Curry, Currey, ——   87
Cuthbertson, Rev. —— 22

D

Dake, Elias   72
Daniel, Daniles, Danills,
   Domiles,
   Margaret   101
   Robert (or Domiles) 100
   William   95
Daragh, George   58
Dare, William   68

Darwin, Kenneth   29
David, John   100
Davidson, ——   56
   William   68
Davis, Harman or Harmon 54, 62
   Henry   64
   Lewis   70
   Thomas   76
   Van   62
   Zachariah   67
Dealey, Alex.   61
Debit, Owen   53
Delchaux, Jacob   95
De Le Chaux, Jacob 99
Delmar, Henry   44
Denem, Charles   101
Densmore, David   56
Dial, Margaret   48, 49
   William   49
Dick, Charles   87
Dickey, Dicky, Alexander 93
   Jane   93
   John   30, 93
Dickson, Jacob   72
   Mickel   73
   Dr. R. J.   5, 27, 28
   Samuel   94
Dies, John   54
Dildinas, Herman   86
Disicker, Jacob   72
Dixon, George   97
Dobbin, Rev. ——   22
Domiles, Daniles, Robert 100
Donegail, Lord   2, 5
Dougherty, John   100
Douglas, Duglass, Duglis,
   Alexander   70, 71
   Elizabeth   70
   Hugh   46
   Margaret   70
   Samuel   70
   William   70
Downes, Jonathon   95
Downy, John   92
Doyall, Hastings   60
   Rebecca, Mrs.   60
Drake, Elias   72
Draper, Dr. Lyman 4, 88
Drennan, Donald   79
Drennen, John   70
   Thos.   79

G

Galaspy, Gelaspie, James	60
John	60, 77
Sara	60
Thomas	60
Gamble, Samuel	75
Ganter, George	97
Ganters, Michael	69
Garden, James	65
Garet, Garret, Elisha	50, 72
Thos.	48
Gaston, Alexander	77
Hugh	79
John	42, 62
Mary	42, 56, 79
Gaunt, Isreal	52
Gervais, John Lewis	94
Wm.	93
Gibbons, Nicholas	66
Gibeney, Gibeny, Martha	68
Gibson, George	70
Jacob	76
James	61, 66
Janet	85
Jean	66
Joseph	61, 66, 74
Margaret	66, 70
Martha	66
Robert	70
Thomas	66
William	66
Gilders, ——	85
Gill, Abraham	50
James M.	75
John	73
Gillies, James	28, 33, 34
Gilmore, John	46, 56
Gilston, Samuel	49
Givens, John	53
Gladney, Joseph	56
Richard	23
Glenry, J. W. and G.	28
Gordon, Mrs. Agnes Beard	55
Jane	55
Moses	69
Thomas	72
Gore, Clement	48
Gorley, Hugh	97
Graber, Cristan	93
Gracey, Gracy, James	68
John	68
Joseph	71

Mary	68
Robert	68
Gray, Archibald	67
Jacob	75
Thomas	67
Green, Daniel	91
Francis	50
Joseph	65
Greg, Gregg, Jane	45
Jean	45
John	35, 45
Mary	59
Ninian	58
William	35, 59
Grendel, John	89
Grieves, John	66
Grimbs, Andrew	80
David	43, 74
Jean	81
Matthew	50, 72, 81
Grodlick, Richard	74
Groghorn, William	99
Gross, Mariah Elizabeth	56
Grumbs, Andrew	80
Guthrie, William	63

H

Hadden, Hadin, Robert	31, 90
Hagel, Henry	59
Haigwood, Buckner	53
Hall, John	99
Samuel	76
Halladay, Samuel	73, 82
Ham, Jeremiah	52
Hambleton, William	76
Hamilton, Charles	97
James	53
John	73, 81
Robert	69
Hannah, or Hanna,	
Agnes	64
Robert	35, 52
Widow	82
Harberson, James	75
Harbison, Agness	79
Hardyman, Thomas	65
Harper, Alexander	66
Jas.	45
William	50
Harport, Mary	61
Harris, William	45
Harse, John	100

McGarragh, Rev. James	23
McGill, Roger	75
McGraw, David	77
Edward	61
McGreary, Edward	97
McGuirts, John	57
McHughes, James	44
McIntosh, John	73
Mr. ———	82
McKane, Kelly	79
McKay, Samuel	96
McKee, Alexander	65
James	66, 91
Jean	91
John	91
Martha	91
Thomas	91, 95
Samuel	61, 74
W.	69
William	91, 99
McKeen, William	74
McKenley, Agnes	55
McKewn, Archibald	58
John	58
Mary	58
McKinly, Agnes	55
McKinney, Roger, Jr.	88
McKnight, McNight, Betsy	95
Eleanor	95
Isabella	95
Jane	98
John	95
Margaret	99
Mary	95, 98
Robert	71, 95
Sarah	95
McKoun, John	58
McKown, Archibald	58
McLelan, John	45
McLelland, Charles	66
Rose	53
Thomas	95
William	52, 53
McLenan, John	47
McLinto, see McClintock	
James	91
John	84
Robert	85
Timothy	82
William	85
McLurken, M'Lurkam, see also	
McClurken,	
Elanor	48

James	35, 47
Jane	48
Lillias	48
Mary	47
Richard	35
Samuel	47
McMachon, McMahon, Arthur	98
McMaster, George	57
Hugh	57
James	76
John	57
Margaret Killock	57
Martha	58
Mary	57
Patrick	57
Thomas	76
William	57, 64
McMichael, Patrick	52
McMillan, John	18
McMillen, Hugh	45
McMullen, Alexander	60
Daniel	69
Hugh	58
McMullins, Mr. ———	94
McMurray, John	65, 78
McMurty, William	47
McNary, Alex'r	63
Gilbert	35, 45, 63
John	63
McNeel, McNeil, Archibald	35, 60
McNight, see McKnight	
McNutt, And'w	66
McQuatty, Mrs. ———	69
McQuesten, McQuestin,	
McQuestine, McQuestion,	
McQuiston,	
David	35, 49
James	35, 44, 45, 49
McQuillen, McQuillion,	
McQuillon,	
John	35, 50
Martha	51
Mary	50
McRee, see McCree	
McRory, Adam	47
Molly	75
McVickar, James	27, 30
McWilliams, Archibald	35, 46
Hugh	44
Janet	51

N

Nagwares, John	85

INDEX OF RIVERS

134   SCOTCH-IRISH MIGRATION TO SOUTH CAROLINA

Cane Creek, waters of
   Tyger River   45, 92, 96, 101
Canes   55
Cane Savannah Branch   97
Caney Creek, waters of Tiger
   River   101
Cannan Creek   52, 56, 59
Cannon(s) Creek   63, 77
Catfish   71
Catawba, Cautawba, Cawtaba
   River   44, 64, 66, 71
Cedar Creek, Craven Co.
   (?)   54, 66, 68, 74, 77
Cedar Creek, Camden Dist. 84, 100
Cedar Creek,
   see also Seader Creek
Charleston, ———Road   73, 88
Cherokee, ———Creek,
   ———Ford   50, 98
Chester Co. 42, 44, 45, 46, 53, 56, 83
Clarenden Co.   64
Clarks Ford of Bullocks
   Creek   68, 69
Coffee Town Creek (see also
   Cuffee Town)   73
Cold Beards Fork   45
Colesons Branch
   (see also Calison's)   58
Colleton Co.   48, 58, 74, 88-91,
   97, 99, 100, 101
Congaree River   60, 72, 77, 78
Connors Creek   43
Cow Creek   60
Craven Co.   43, 46-49, 50-59,
   60, 63-65, 67-69, 70-79, 80-87,
   89, 90-99, 100-101
Cuffee Town, waters of
   (see also Coffee Town)   81

D
Daniels Branch   95
Dry Branch, of Cedar Creek   77
Dry Creek, waters of Cawtaba 44
Dry Creek, of Mine Creek,
   Waters of Little Saluda   99
Dry Fork of Dutchmans Creek   65
Dudleys Creek   79, 81
Duncans, Dunkens, Dunkings,
   Dunkins,
   Creek 45, 51, 63, 82, 93, 94

Durbins Creek   42, 48, 59
Dutchmans Creek, Dry Fork of 65

E
Eight-mile Branch of Gills
   Creek   51, 52
Enoree River   47, 48, 49, 51,
   54, 59, 64, 69, 72, 85, 86, 90, 93,
   97, 99

F
Fair Forest   77, 78, 80
Fairview Church   83
Ferguson, Forguson Creek,
   waters of
   Tiger River   83, 84, 100
Flat Creek   68
Fishing Creek   42, 45,
   46, 77, 79, 82, 92
Four Holes,
   waters of   51, 64, 65, 71, 99

G
Gastons Branch of Turkey
   Creek   56
Gilders Creek   85
Gilkeys Creek   99
Gills, Gils Creek, north side of
   Santee River   51, 52
Gills, Gils Creek, Waxhaw
   Settlement   55, 62, 63, 73, 77
Granas, Grannys,
   Quarter   50, 69, 97, 99
Granville Co.   46, 57, 58, 64, 67,
   72, 74, 82, 84, 88, 96, 97, 101
Great Flat Rock Creek   97
Great Lynches Creek   58
Greenville District   83

H
Hanging Rock, ———Branch,
   ———Creek   55, 99
Hannahs Creek   55, 62
Hauts Branch, waters of
   Little River   62
Hays Branch   46
Hendricks Branch of Dunkins
   Creek   82
Hendrick's Creek, branch of
   Indian Creek   49
Hillsborough Township 95, 98, 99

www.ingramcontent.com/pod-product-compliance
Lightning Source LLC
Chambersburg PA
CBHW061749270326
41928CB00011B/2431